VH1 Music First BEHIND THE MUSIC: THE DAY THE MUSIC DIED

MARTIN HUXLEY AND QUINTON SKINNER

POCKET BOOKS

New York   London   Toronto   Sydney   Singapore

An *Original* Publication of POCKET BOOKS

Music First

POCKET BOOKS, a division of Simon & Schuster, Inc.
1230 Avenue of the Americas, New York, NY 10020

ISBN: 0-671-03962-8

First Pocket Books trade paperback printing
November 2000

10 9 8 7 6 5 4 3 2 1

POCKET and colophon are registered trademarks of
Simon & Schuster, Inc.

Interior and cover design by Matt Bouloutian and
Andrea Sepic/Red Herring Design

Printed in the U.S.A.

Photo and Footage Credits

WPA Film Library (pages 3, 70); Bill Griggs/Rockin' 50s
Magazine (pages 4, 12, 14, 22-23, 26, 33, 39, 43, 47,
60-61, 65, 68, 73, 76, 81, 106, 121); Bob Keane
(pages 6, 53); Louise Rasdale/Rex USA (pages
10, 90-91, 94-95) J. P. Richardson (son of the Big Bopper)
(pages 16, 34, 36, 89, 108-109, 113, 114,119); Show
Time Music Archive (Toronto) (page 18); Tony Szikil
(pages 21, 50); Ernestine Reyes (pages 28, 29, 57, 82);
Donna Fox (pages 31, 32); Fish Films, Inc. (page 55);
Gil Rocha (page 58); Alan Clark (page 89)

Front and back cover art : UPI/Corbis/Bettman

BEHIND THE MUSIC™
THE DAY
THE MUSIC
DIED

VH1 Music First

MARTIN HUXLEY AND QUINTON SKINNER

THE DAY THE MUSIC DIED

✵

Clear Lake, Iowa, isn't a big town. Des Moines is to the south, Minneapolis to the north; neither one is really very close. The farmer's fields are never more than a few minutes' drive away. In the winter the snows come and blanket the landscape, and you feel as though everything in the world is someplace else, and too far for you to reach.

It's 1959. Early February in northern Iowa. For a teenager like you, it's that long post-holiday stretch before spring and—could it come fast enough?—summer vacation. There aren't many diversions for you in this small town in the Midwest. Life for a young person is devoted to school, family, friends, church, and high-school sports. Oh, and the radio.

You see, in the last few years something different has come along. A new kind of music called rock 'n' roll. It's being condemned by parents and politicians. They say it incites the spirits of young people, that it encourages mixing of the races and licentiousness. Kids who listen to rock 'n' roll music dance and shout, and God knows what might happen.

Exactly.

But what the parents don't seem to understand is that the kids who listen to rock 'n' roll music aren't all looking to go against the grain of society—at least not in the obvious manner that their parents imagine. Rock 'n' roll is about energy and freedom. It's not about doing wrong—it's about the moment. And that feels so *right*. Rock 'n' roll speaks to you as you're riding the storms between your childhood and adulthood; the songs sound like they were written just for you. Its stars are exotic and interesting, beautiful young men like Elvis and the charming African-American sophisticate Chuck Berry.

Rock 'n' roll music gets the kids stirred up, that's for sure.

Some people say the music is a fad, that it's due to die out any day now. Its greatest stars have fallen to military service, scandal, and career eclipse. The day Elvis left for the army you felt a sense of loss, just like your friends. But there are new stars on the way, and the radio brings you the fresh sounds that kids in the big cities are into. Clear Lake starts to feel like it's connected to the great big world outside.

On February 2, the kids are beside themselves. Something called the Winter Dance Party is coming to town. It's a rock 'n' roll package show, the kind that usually plays the big cities—and It's coming to Clear Lake. You can barely believe it. All day KRIB radio plays songs by the stars who are going to appear that night at the Surf Ballroom: the Big Bopper, Ritchie Valens, Buddy Holly.

You walk around all day at school singing their songs: "That'll Be the Day"; "La Bamba"—the one with the Spanish words you don't understand; and "Chantilly Lace."

This is the highlight of a teenager's year in Clear Lake, Iowa, in 1959. Buddy Holly, Ritchie Valens, and the Big Bopper are the leading lights of rock 'n' roll. It would be a very bad time to be grounded—but you're not, and you scraped together enough money for a ticket. All your friends are going to be there. At the high school the kids are whispering in the hallways. You feel like shouting for joy when the final bell rings.

There's a big crowd outside the Surf Ballroom waiting to get in. When you come through the doors, you're suspended for an instant between the cold air outside and the harm humidity that's starting to build up inside. And then you forget the cold. You forget everything except the night ahead.

You look around. The Surf Ballroom is made for ballroom dancing. The walls are painted to look like a tropical beach. Looking up, you see stars twinkling on the ceiling. The stage is lit up, and soon the first act will appear. More than a thousand teenagers pack the place. The kids are saying to each other: This is the biggest thing to hit Clear Lake. *Ever.*

The tour bus pulls across the gravel parking lot. They've arrived. Clear Lake, Iowa. The Surf Ballroom. This isn't a scheduled stop, it was an open date on the tour that was filled by the bookers at the last minute. The musicians probably figure they might as well make as much money as they can, take a paying gig where it presents itself, because the Winter Dance Party sure as hell hasn't been a picnic on the beach.

To begin with, it's cold. *Really* cold. It's the dead of winter in the upper Midwest. A lot of guys on this bus have never felt temperatures like this in their entire lives. And, to make matters worse, they've been traveling on cheap, broken-down old school buses. They've been riding hundreds of miles a day across the frozen landscape, the buses breaking down, the heaters breaking down. Their bus broke down a few days ago and one of them got frostbite, for God's sake. He's still in the hospital.

Buddy's having money problems because of a hassle with his former manager. That's why he's on the tour in the first place—he says he's trying to start up a record label, get into the business side of things. He says that's where the smart money is. Buddy and the Bopper are on the phone every day to their pregnant wives—Buddy's in New York, the Bopper's in Texas. They're all homesick. Ritchie is just a kid, alone and far away from home for the first time.

Still, it's a show. And these guys love the music they play. They love to be on stage, to feel the energy of the crowd and to just *let go* for a little while. They get off the bus and the cold wind hits them. There's a whisper of snow in the air. They pull up their collars and run for the door of the Surf Ballroom. The wind picks up and even Buddy's pomaded hair is flying around everyplace.

Oh, man, one of them says. *It's so cold.*

The Winter Dance Party tour hasn't been all bad. Any of them will tell you that. The shows have all been really good, and they're a bunch of regular guys. They've stuck together instead of being pulled apart by the nasty conditions. They watch each other play, try to learn a thing or two. Musicians are competitive people, but when they all love the music they learn to appreciate each other. They've got some good people on this tour, that's for sure.

The show that night is like a party. The crowd presses the stage and dances and screams. Your throat hurts from hollering.

Man, this is good music. The Big Bopper comes out—he's a big man, with an outsized personality you can feel all the way to the back of the room. The Bopper sweats under the

BUDDY AND THE BOPPER ARE

ON THE PHONE

EVERY DAY TO

THEIR PREGNANT

WIVES—BUDDY'S IN NEW YORK,

THE BOPPER'S IN TEXAS.

THEY'RE ALL HOMESICK.

RITCHIE IS JUST

A KID, ALONE

AND FAR AWAY FROM HOME

FOR THE FIRST TIME.

lights, looks unsteady for a second but then a big smile breaks open across his face. He takes the microphone and says, "Heeellloooo baaaaaabeeee!" and the kids go wild. Everyone's tapping their toes and singing along.

Buddy Holly's on stage. Buddy looks tall and gangly, and he wears thick glasses. He doesn't look like one of the popular kids at school, but when he starts singing he's so sure of himself that the girls all stare up at him like he was the star quarterback. When he sings "Weh-helll that'll be the day . . . woo-hoo!" the place is rockin'. Who cares how cold it is out-side? Buddy reels off great song after great song. The kids know all the words.

And then Ritchie Valens plays. He's just a kid, the same age as you. And he takes over the place.

Ritchie sings, "Para bailar La Bamba, Bamba se necesita una poca de gracia . . . " and it's like a riot in there—but a good kind. It's hard to explain, for a teenager in the Surf Ballroom. You feel so good, it's like you never want to forget this moment. Your heart is beating hard and fast in your chest, you're clapping your hands and screaming and laughing. This *is* the best thing ever.

A WARM BED, A HOT MEAL, CLEAN CLOTHES.

THAT'S WHAT THEY'RE ALL THINKING ABOUT, BUDDY, RITCHIE, AND THE BIG BOPPER.

THE PLANE STARTS UP THE RUNWAY, BUILDS UP SPEED, AND LEAVES THE GROUND.

A FEW MINUTES LATER

THE SNOWS COME IN TO CLEAR LAKE.

IT'S PRETTY BAD,

A WORSE STORM THAN ANYONE HAD EXPECTED.

Backstage, Buddy's had enough. The show the next night is in Moorhead, Minnesota. Look at a map. Moorhead. All the way up there. That means another long night on the bus freezing their asses off. They've been spending all the time on the bus or on stage. They haven't even had time to wash their clothes. They don't need coat hangers—their shirts are so dirty they can stand up in the closet on their own.

Buddy has an idea. He asks the manager of the Surf Ballroom if he can get him in touch with a charter flight service. Buddy wants to hire a plane to Fargo, where he and his band can sleep in warm beds and wash their clothes before tomorrow night's show.

It sounds like heaven. *Oh, man.* A nice clean bed, a hot meal, clothes right out of the dryer.

The Big Bopper gets wind of this. He's sick with the flu, he's got a fever, and he's really been suffering on the bus. He's too big to get comfortable in those little seats. He finds Buddy's bass player and asks him if he can have his seat on the flight.

The young man looks at the Bopper and shrugs. *Sure,* he says. *It's all right with me if it's all right with Buddy.*

In the hallway outside the dressing room, Buddy's guitar player is dealing with Ritchie Valens. Ritchie's been pestering him ever since they found out about the flight. Ritchie wants to get on the flight. He *really* wants to get on the plane. Finally the guitar player has had enough.

Look, he says, *I'll flip you for it.*

They flip a coin. Ritchie calls heads. Ritchie wins.

In the dressing room, Buddy learns that his bass player has given up his seat on the airplane to the Bopper. Buddy is leaning back and laughing.

I hope you freeze your ass off on that bus, he says.

The bass player grins and shakes his head. *Well, I hope your plane crashes.*

The Surf Ballroom manager drives the guys to the airport after midnight. They're nice people; they talk on the way about where they're all from. When they reach the airport they drive right up to the plane, which is waiting on the runway. The pilot's been going back and forth with the control tower. There's snow in the air, a problem with visibility. For a minute it's unclear what they're going to do. Finally they decide to go.

There are only four seats on the little plane. Buddy sits in front, right next to the pilot. He loves to fly, and he'll probably chat with the pilot the whole way up to Fargo. Ritchie and the Bopper squeeze into the back. The door is closed.

A warm bed, a hot meal, clean clothes. That's what they're all thinking about, Buddy, Ritchie, and the Big Bopper.

The plane starts up the runway, builds up speed, and leaves the ground. A few minutes later the snows come in to Clear Lake. It's pretty bad, a worse storm than anyone had expected.

The DJ who was Master of Ceremonies at the Surf Ballroom that night is driving home.

The snow is blowing in a straight line across his windshield. He turns to his wife and says, *I hope the guys got off the ground.*

The Surf Ballroom manager pauses in his car. He had been watching the plane's lights going up into the sky. But then he thought he'd seen the lights going down.

No, it had to be an illusion. Can't be.

The next morning you're listening to KRIB, eating your breakfast, when you get the news. Your jaw drops open, and you don't believe it at first.

They're all dead. Buddy, Ritchie, and the Big Bopper. Their plane went down right outside of Clear Lake.

You stand there, your arms hanging at your sides, and you just feel your heart beating hard in your chest for a while. *How can it still be beating,* you ask yourself, *when it's just been broken?*

THE NEXT MORNING **YOU'RE LISTENING** TO KRIB, EATING YOUR BREAKFAST, WHEN YOU GET

THE NEWS.

YOUR JAW DROPS

OPEN, AND YOU DON'T BELIEVE IT AT FIRST. THEY'RE

ALL DEAD.

BUDDY, RITCHIE, AND THE BIG BOPPER.

THAT'LL BE THE DAY

The Iowa plane crash that killed Buddy Holly, Ritchie Valens, J. P. Richardson (The Big Bopper), and pilot Roger Peterson during the predawn hours of February 3, 1959, stands as a pivotal moment in the history of American culture.

The country lost three of its most popular performers, and a generation marked the end of rock 'n' roll's youthful innocence and optimism. The Day the Music Died—as it was immortalized in Don McLean's 1972 hit "American Pie"—brought the harsh realities of life and death to the brash promise of rock 'n' roll. The music was never the same again.

In the years since, the plane crash has taken on the air of legend, but at the time it was a very real tragedy whose consequences resonate still among fans, music lovers, and the people who knew the three star-crossed rockers as friends, family, and colleagues. Even today, their voices reveal the pain and shock of that day. The rest of us are left with the compelling image of three dynamic artists preserved in their youth, never to fall victim to career decline or the artistic embarrassments that would eventually catch up with their contemporaries,

never to end up as dinosaurs treading the boards of the oldies circuit. Their music lives on to crystallize a moment in time that was stopped like a needle being lifted off a record.

Buddy Holly was just twenty-two years old when he died, but in his short life he was instrumental in elevating rock music as an art form and as a vehicle for personal expression. He was a compelling performer, a distinctive stylist, and an inventive sonic architect. What's more, his music *rocked.* He was a strong-willed artist with a clear-eyed musical vision and an increasingly unshakable determination to do things his own way. At the time of his death he was preparing to embark upon an ambitious new phase of his career, working behind the scenes with other artists while continuing to expand the range of his own creativity through recording.

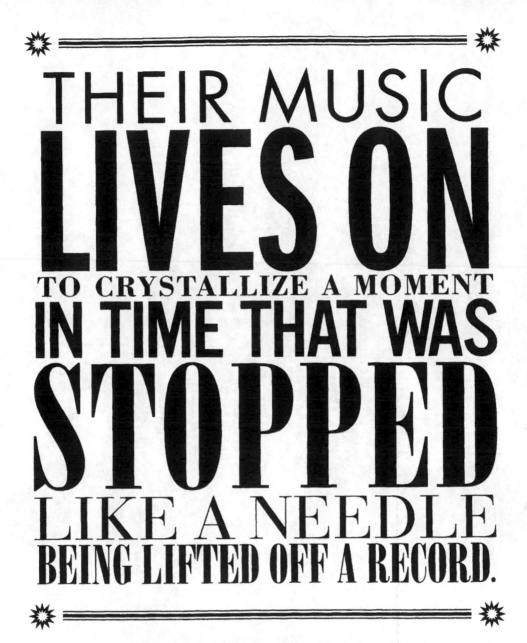

THEIR MUSIC LIVES ON TO CRYSTALLIZE A MOMENT IN TIME THAT WAS STOPPED LIKE A NEEDLE BEING LIFTED OFF A RECORD.

Ritchie Valens was only seventeen when he died; his recording career lasted a scant eight months. He released only three singles, but it's hard today to name another rocker who made such a major impact with such a slight body of work. Valens was rock's first Latino star, and he blazed a trail for Hispanic artists that has been walked by many. When he died, Ritchie was widely regarded as one of

the music's most promising stars, a raw yet engaging rocker who was poised to build on his overnight success.

The Big Bopper was twenty-nine when he died in the plane crash; at the time he was basking in the glory of recording one of the international smash records of the year. J. P. Richardson was a Texas disk jockey with boundless energy and a knack for crafting

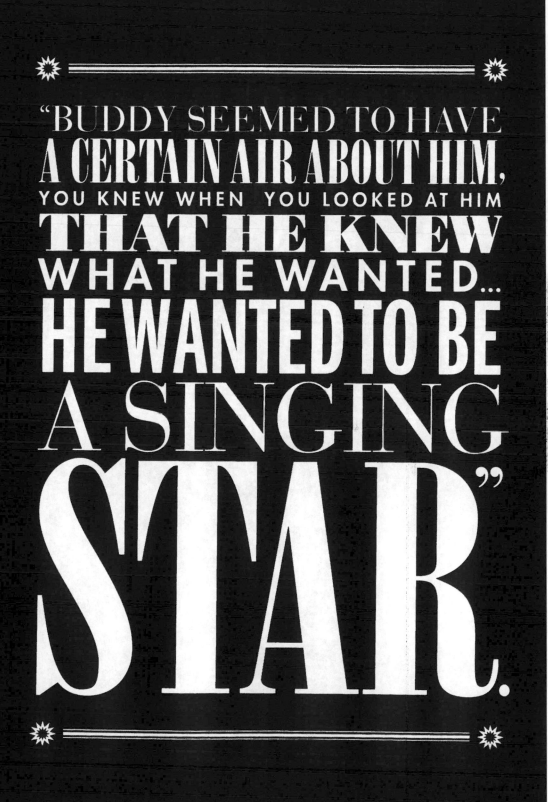

"BUDDY SEEMED TO HAVE A CERTAIN AIR ABOUT HIM, YOU KNEW WHEN YOU LOOKED AT HIM THAT HE KNEW WHAT HE WANTED... HE WANTED TO BE A SINGING STAR."

memorable songs that blossomed into a recording career. His flair for entertaining listeners on the radio spawned his bigger-than-life alter ego, the Big Bopper. While the boisterous, fun-loving Bopper embodied rock 'n' roll's unleashed and unhinged spirit, J. P.'s more conventional songwriting efforts revealed a sensitive and romantic soul.

Rock 'n' roll's early years were turbulent and crazy. The convergence of country-and-western with black rhythm-and-blues came to life on the night of July 5, 1954, when an unknown Memphis teenager named Elvis Presley laid down his debut single "That's All Right" in the tiny Sun studio. This new music struck an instant chord among America's young people. Unlike the sanitary and conformist pop styles that preceded it, rock 'n' roll had an edge of danger, rebellion, and open sexuality. It was just what the doctor ordered, and the teens of the day would become the first generation of American youth to totally reject their parents' musical tastes.

And who could blame them? The adults reviled the music as a blatant inducement to racial openness and sexual abandon. *And they were right.*

But by the late '50s, rock's vitality had been sapped by a series of setbacks. Elvis was in the army. Jerry Lee Lewis had touched off a scandal when he married his thirteen-year-old cousin. Little Richard had abandoned rock 'n' roll for the ministry. Suddenly the music was in the hands of a second wave of stars—and among the best and brightest were Buddy Holly, Ritchie Valens, and the Big Bopper.

When that plane crashed in Iowa, it felt like the music really had died. But rock was strong enough to withstand even the loss of three of its earliest pioneers—and it would always bear the imprint of their legacy.

Buddy Holly was a uniquely gifted musical pioneer whose innovations helped chart the course of rock 'n' roll as we know it today. He also had a natural gift for singing and playing the guitar, and his classic recordings embody the best of rock's exuberance and optimism.

Holly was a versatile craftsman who balanced yearning romanticism with sly humor; as a result, he spoke directly to the emotional lives of his teenage listeners. He was also restless and driven, and his fascination with the recording process yielded sonic innovations such as original echo techniques, overdubbing, and double-tracking. His use of the quartet lineup in the Crickets as a self-contained unit directly inspired four English boys who followed his lead and formed the Beatles.

Niki Sullivan (guitar, the Crickets): "Buddy seemed to have a certain air about him, you knew when you looked at him that he knew what he wanted. . . . He wanted to be a singing star . . . when you looked into his eyes you just knew—he wants it. He knows what he wants. And you have to appreciate that, no matter who you are."

Buddy was the first rocker with the commercial clout to gain artistic control over his recordings, and he had the talent to take advantage of that freedom. He was one of the first rock musicians to write his own songs, and he synthesized a sound that remains distinctive more then forty years later.

Unlike virtually every other '50s rocker, the gangly bespectacled Holly had no preten-sions of being either a sex symbol or a wild-eyed outlaw. Elvis was exotic, seemingly untouchable. Buddy was unassuming and approachable. He seemed more like a friend than a deity.

Niki Sullivan: "Buddy was just a good old boy. Just a doggone nice guy. He was your next-door neighbor. He could be a brother, could be a cousin, a friend.

He was thin, wore glasses. Curled his hair, did things that we all did in the '50s; anything to be noticed, to be recognized, to have others' attention, if you will. But personally speaking to Buddy Holly you got the impression that he was a little bit quiet, a little bit shy."

Ritchie Valens shared Buddy's shy sincerity, but he also shared his quietly cocky ambition. Ritchie rose up out of poverty to become a star, and his drive to provide for his family drove his musical ambition. He was a magnetic performer whose recordings suggest a talent still in its formative stages. His music featured a balance of raw immediacy and focused craftsmanship. He was equally comfortable with gritty rockers as with romantic ballads. He also had yet to see his eighteenth birthday.

Connie Lemos (Ritchie Valens's sister): "He was warm. Very, very warm. He was funny . . . my mother, at seventy-two years old when we lost her, had the heart of a child . . . and Ritchie was the same way. No matter how hard life got, my mom always told us, 'Look at the bright side. It can only get better.' Ritchie was just very positive . . . and I think part of the legacy he left for us was just that he set a goal, and nothing would stop him until he attained it."

"**BUDDY**
WAS JUST A GOOD OLD BOY.
JUST A DOGGONE
NICE GUY.
HE WAS YOUR NEXT-DOOR NEIGHBOR.
HE COULD BE A BROTHER,
COULD BE A COUSIN,
A FRIEND"

Donna Fox

(namesake of Ritchie's hit "Donna"):

"We had dances at school . . . and we always danced together. He was a wonderful dancer. I thought he was cute. His eyes were hazel, and his hair was very, very dark. And he had a little bit of freckles over his nose, just a little . . . he was cute, and he was so nice. He was so pleasant, just his mannerisms. . . . He just knew he was going to be a star, and he was going to have a cabinet full of his gold records. That was what he kept talking about."

J. P. Richardson was a natural entertainer. He had a garrulous charm and a broad sense of humor that filled a room as effectively as his burly physique. He was also a devoted family man and a gifted songwriter with a more serious side that might have won him greater fame if his career hadn't been cut short.

The Big Bopper was *fun*. It was impossible to see him on stage, or hear him on record, and not smile while your foot started tapping.

Jerry Boynton (friend of J. P.'s):

"He was a very humble person. And, to some extent, he was a loner. He selected friends carefully. He was very gregarious. His true persona was retreating to write music, retreating to very close friends . . . and so the Big Bopper, that was all show. I think you'd have to agree he gave it his all as the Big Bopper, but J. P. Richardson was a very humble person . . . I recall this story about his doing a performance. Alan Freed, the great disk jockey of the day, introduced him in Chicago. He said, 'To many he's the Big Bopper, but I want you to know he's also Mr. Nice Guy.' And that's what he was."

All three men are invariably described as down-to-earth, gracious, and driven by their ambition.

Travis Holley (Buddy's brother):

"Buddy was very driven. He acted like he didn't have enough time to do what he wanted to do. He was always in a hurry, and very tense and nervous most of the time. He was a very shy person but when he got to doing something that he enjoyed doing well, he just seemed to settle down and a peaceful calm came over him then. But until he attained that, he was very intense and nervous and it seemed like he was looking for something, looking for satisfaction of some kind. And I don't believe he ever did anything that he thought was good enough. I think he was trying constantly to better himself in whatever he chose to do."

Buddy was born Charles Hardin Holley on September 7, 1936, in Lubbock, Texas. Lubbock was a conservative, deeply Christian town, and liquor was banned from its public places until 1972. As a result, a string of honky-tonks and liquor stores waited just past the city limits.

Buddy was the youngest of Ella and Lawrence Odell Holley's four children. Ella and L. O., as he was known to his friends, raised their three oldest children during the depths of the Great Depression, with the industrious L. O. working as a carpenter, cook, tailor, and even as a boxing-ring timekeeper to make ends meet. By all accounts, the Holleys were a loving, hard-working Baptist family, and Ella and L. O. passed on their strong work ethic to their children.

The Holley household resonated with the sound of church music and hillbilly country. Even when money was scarce, the Holleys always managed to pay for their children's music lessons. Buddy's older brothers Larry and Travis each played several instruments, and they often performed as a duo at social functions and talent contests.

When he was five, Buddy won a five-dollar prize at a local talent show for singing and

clutching a toy fiddle. He took an active interest in music when he was in his early teens, studying piano and steel guitar before he decided that he'd rather play acoustic guitar like his big brother Travis. Soon enough he was also proficient on banjo and mandolin.

Travis Holley:

"Well, actually I taught him his first chords on the guitar. It was a little bit hard to do, because we had just the one guitar and we'd pass it back and forth. I'd show him a chord and then hand it to him . . . it didn't take long, though. He was a quick study and he learned fast. In fact, before long he was showing *me* new things. . . . He wasn't content just to play four chords in a song like I would. He'd say, 'There's another chord that goes in there, Trav.' And I'd say, 'Well, we can fake it and get by with that.' But now he wants to learn that other chord. And so he would learn it. And I guess that's what it takes."

Buddy entered high school in 1949. He and his friends listened to the country-and-western music of the day—in particular, the maverick singer-songwriter Hank Williams.

Buddy formed a performing duo with friend Jack Neal; Buddy and Jack got a big break when they performed on local radio. Their performances were so impressive that they were given a weekly slot on KDAV's *Sunday Party* in 1953. Buddy saw that the station's facilities could be used as a recording studio, and cut a two-song acetate with Jack. Buddy also formed a partnership with high-school friend Bob Montgomery, making demo recordings and writing songs.

Buddy's bands went through various personnel changes and lineups. They were no different from the countless garage bands that Buddy would eventually inspire. They were mainly playing country and bluegrass music, tuning into the radio late at night to listen to influential live country shows such as Nashville's *Grand Ole Opry*, Dallas's *Big D Jamboree*, and Shreveport's *Louisiana Hayride*.

Travis Holley:

"All of them would encourage each other, and they'd get together and jam, and they thought they were unbeatable. Every time there was a new grocery store or a furniture mart or anything like that—a grand opening—they would go

there to play. Just to do it for free and get the exposure. And they thought if they got enough exposure, they would be on the road to greatness. They had cards printed up, they would play at high-school proms and for anybody that would hire them. And it seemed to pay off."

Lubbock in the '50s was as racially segregated as any Southern city, but societal constraints couldn't keep Buddy and his friends from listening to black rhythm-and-blues on the radio. Late at night they tuned in to faraway stations on their car radios, starting up the engine and moving whenever the signal started to fade. Buddy got into R&B artists like Hank Ballard and the Midnighters, Jackie Wilson, the Drifters and the Dominoes, as well as harder-edged electric bluesmen such as Howlin' Wolf, Little Walter, and Muddy Waters. This music was grittier and more aggressive than the country and bluegrass they were familiar with, and new musical ideas started to percolate in Buddy's fertile mind.

The same thing was going on all around the country. Radio brought exotic and dangerous sounds to young and impressionable ears, especially in the segregated South. The language of music was beginning to break down barriers in the minds of the young.

Niki Sullivan:
"When Buddy started playing music at thirteen, he played strictly country music. That kind of music was really all we had until about 1953, '54, when we started searching the dial of the radio to see what else was going on out there."

Buddy and Bob Montgomery became full-time radio partners in late 1954; they incorporated a bass, guitar, and fiddle, and began to detour into blues and R&B alongside their country repertoire. They began billing their sound as "Western and Bop." Buddy began writing more and more blues and R&B songs for the group, and he sang lead on his own songs. He and his friends started to venture into the black side of town to see local bluesmen. Buddy carefully watched the black guitar players and learned to emulate blues playing.

Buddy's consciousness opened up, and he questioned the racial prejudices of the time.

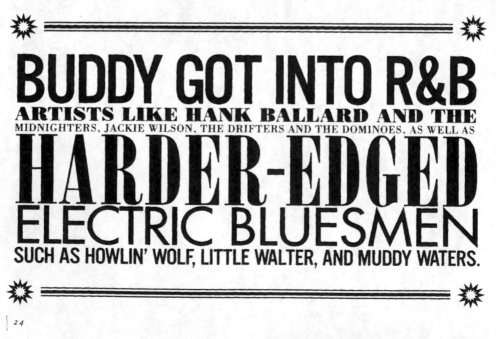

BUDDY GOT INTO R&B
ARTISTS LIKE HANK BALLARD AND THE
MIDNIGHTERS, JACKIE WILSON, THE DRIFTERS AND THE DOMINOES, AS WELL AS
HARDER-EDGED
ELECTRIC BLUESMEN
SUCH AS HOWLIN' WOLF, LITTLE WALTER, AND MUDDY WATERS.

In his mind, music was tearing away the barriers between the races. Eventually he would name his pet cat after the African-American reformer and educator Booker T. Washington. His boldest statement as a teenage integrationist was bringing home visiting hero Little Richard—whose sexually charged presence caused a minor scandal wherever he went—for dinner with his parents.

Buddy and Bob Montgomery played local country-and-western clubs, and opened up shows on KDAV for visiting performers. In early 1955, Buddy and Bob were in the audience when Elvis Presley played a show in Lubbock. He played twice more in Lubbock that year, and Buddy and Bob gave Elvis a tour of their hometown.

Travis Holley:

"I believe Buddy became very impatient when he saw other fellows about his age breaking into music, like Elvis Presley and the Everly Brothers. He believed he could play along with any of them, and I'm pretty sure he could."

Bob Montgomery:

"Meeting Elvis was what really inspired Buddy to get things going."

Buddy was easy-going, almost shy. But he was also driven and self-assured, with a cocky confidence that could border on arrogance. He had a darker, brooding side that sometimes perplexed his friends. Family members recall him jamming with his friends at the Holley home and berating them when he felt they weren't taking the music seriously enough. He went on solitary late-night drives to work on his songs in his head and organize his musical ideas.

Record companies realized that rock 'n' roll was the trend of the day. They saw the mountain of money that Elvis was making for his company, and scrambled to cash in. Decca Records's Nashville office offered to sign Buddy as a solo artist; his initial inclination was to turn down the offer and stay loyal to his group, but Bob Montgomery urged his friend not to let this opportunity slip away. Buddy accepted the Decca deal—and took on a new stage name when Decca accidentally dropped the "e" from his last name on the contract he signed.

Buddy put together a new band with pals Sonny Curtis, Don Guess, and Jerry Allison. He got his first taste of the realities of the music business when he and his sidemen arrived at Bradley's Barn studio in Nashville to cut a record with famed producer Owen Bradley. Bradley decided that Buddy shouldn't play guitar on the session, and Buddy was forced to hold his tongue when Bradley brought in session men to play guitar and drums.

Decca was a powerful and prestigious label with an impressive country roster. That didn't mean the company had any idea how to make and market rock 'n' roll.

Bill Griggs (Buddy Holly historian and fan):
"Decca Nashville was country. It didn't do rock 'n' roll, and they did not know how to handle Buddy Holly. After he did his very first session, somebody said 'Buddy Holly is the biggest no-talent I've ever worked with.' They had a country band behind him and they were trying to make him sing country-style. It was just like the *Buddy Holly Story* movie with Gary Busey, except Buddy never hit his producer. He sort of wished he had, because then Buddy could have done what he wanted to do. After the Decca sessions in Nashville were a failure, Buddy came back to Lubbock."

COME ON LET'S GO

---✸---

While Buddy was struggling to get his career off the ground, young Richard Steven Valenzuela was firmly under the spell of the rock 'n' roll explosion. He built himself a green-and-white electric guitar in wood shop, and filled his days learning to play and fantasizing about joining the ranks of Elvis, Chuck Berry, Bo Diddley, and Little Richard.

Ritohie was born May 13, 1941, in the suburbs of Los Angeles. His father, Steven, was a jack-of-all-trades who worked as a pipe setter, tree surgeon, and horse trainer. His mother Concepcion—Connie for short—had come to California with her family from Arizona roots. She had been married previously and had a son, Bob Morales, who was four years older than Ritchie. Ritchie also had two younger sisters and a younger brother.

Ritchie's family didn't usually speak Spanish in their home, but the Valenzuela house was filled with Mexican folk ballads, *conjunto* tunes, and flamenco and mariachi music. Steve Valenzuela was also a fan of American blues and R&B, and Ritchie grew up absorbing these sounds with a hungry ear. Ritchie lived with his father after his parents separated, but Steve Valenzuela died of complications from diabetes when Ritchie was ten; Connie moved the family into Steve's one-bedroom house in Pacoima. The tiny home often overflowed with relatives, and Ritchie many times spent the night in a sleeping bag in a hollowed-out area underneath the house.

Connie Lemos (Ritchie's younger sister):
"I didn't think it was hard. We didn't know any different. Later on, people used to tell us, 'Oh, you used to be so poor and now you have a nice house.' Our furniture's better now, but we never felt poor. Mama raised us with a lot of dignity, and she always gave us the best she could."

Ritchie never had formal musical training, but he eventually got hold of a battered old guitar and learned some chords from a neighbor. He was a natural lefty, but he was in too much of a hurry to restring the instrument and learned to play right-handed. He began to play at family gatherings and for his school-mates at Pacoima High School. He mixed the traditional Mexican songs of his childhood with his favorite rock songs.

Bob Morales (Ritchie's brother):
"I used to kid him about carrying his guitar with him. He would just nod and smile at me. One day I went down to take him his lunch money and walked to the back of the school. He was underneath a tree, on the lawn, with about ten girls around him, and he was playing his guitar. Clearly, a method to his madness. That was all he did. All he did was play his guitar."

On January 31, 1957, a transport jet and a navy training plane collided in the sky and scattered wreckage over the grounds of Ritchie's school. Three students, including Ritchie's best friend, were killed. Ninety more were injured. Ritchie wasn't in school that day because he was attending his grandfather's funeral.

Bob Morales:
"We had just got back from burying my grand-father. We were standing outside my grand-mother's house when we heard an explosion and I happened to look up and seen this plane going down. We all jumped in the car and went

A young Ritchie with his older brother, Bob.

down to Pacoima Junior High School. It looked like a battlefield out there. There was pieces of airplane and aluminum and engines and kids laying all over the playground. I guess you could say that my grandfather's funeral saved his life. And Ritchie took it kind of hard, you know."

Ritchie's life had been spared—he surely would have been on the playground where the wreckage came down to earth—but the incident instilled in him a fear of flying that haunted him for the rest of his short life.

Donna Fox:

"He would have nightmares about that. He just had a horrible fear of small planes, and planes in general. He indicated that he would never fly, he just would never fly."

Ritchie had a knack for playing guitar and singing. In 1957 he was invited by local band-leader Gil Rocha to play in his band, the Silhouettes. They covered hits at high-school hops, church dances, and private parties. The band was unique in its racial mixture, with African-American and Asian members playing alongside Chicanos. Ritchie soon became one of the group's featured vocalists. It wasn't long before Ritchie was adding his own compositions to the Silhouettes's repertoire.

Gil Rocha:

"He tuned up, started singing, and he just floored me. He really impressed me with his musical talent, his artistry in handling the guitar without even looking. I don't think he ever looked where his guitar was, he just strummed away. When Ritchie would play his music, they would come rushing up to the front of the stage, literally, and just stand there and clap and yell and scream."

Ritchie had real charisma and stage presence. He also showed a sense of adventure in his choice of material, adding a smattering of Mexican songs to the band's rock and R&B set list.

At one of the Silhouettes' neighborhood party gigs, Ritchie met a sixteen-year-old named Donna Ludwig (now Fox). Donna was a pretty blonde who would eventually lend her name to Ritchie's biggest hit.

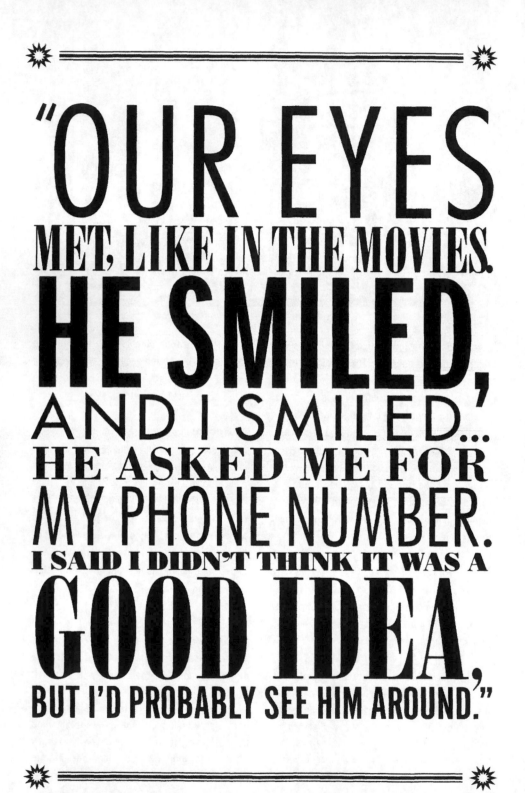

"OUR EYES MET, LIKE IN THE MOVIES. HE SMILED, AND I SMILED... HE ASKED ME FOR MY PHONE NUMBER. I SAID I DIDN'T THINK IT WAS A GOOD IDEA, BUT I'D PROBABLY SEE HIM AROUND."

Donna Fox:

"Our eyes met, like in the movies. He smiled, and I smiled. And then during the break he came over and we started talking. Ritchie came over and asked at the end of the party if I needed a ride home. I told him I had my own car, and he asked me for my phone number. I said I didn't think it was a good idea, but I'd probably see him around. He lived in Pacoima, and I lived over in Granada Hills. It was kind of like the other side of the tracks. So we really didn't mingle in the same groups."

Ritchie and Donna didn't talk for a while, but one day Donna was in the hallway of San Fernando High School when she saw Ritchie. They began talking, and their initial attraction was rekindled. Donna's father didn't approve.

Donna Fox:

"When we went to school we became very close, and we saw each other all the time. I had to sneak out, it was kind of a bad situation because my father didn't want me dating a Mexican boy. It was pretty easy to do, though. I was pretty slick in doing it [laughs]. We went to parties all the time. Most of the time at the parties he entertained, so it interfered a little bit with just being with him all night, you know? But we managed to get to the movies, and go to the park, and have picnics and go for rides and things like that."

Ritchie lived for his music, and he knew he was going to be a star. His mother supported his ambition, using meager resources to help him get instruments and stage clothes.

Gil Rocha:

"After playing for about eight months, a friend of mine had a tape recorder and I asked him if I could use it because I wanted to tape the band. At the end of the show I said, 'Hey, can I

have my tape?' He said, 'No, I'm going to take it. I know this guy in Hollywood who's looking for talent.' So I reluctantly gave it to him. It turned out to be good, because that's how Ritchie got started."

The friend was Doug Macchia, a twenty-two-year-old printer who had just manufactured business cards for producer/musician/entrepreneur Bob Keane. Macchia knew that Keane was looking for artists to sign to his new company, Del-Fi. Macchia brought the rough tape of the Silhouettes's performance to Keane, who was interested enough to check out the band live.

Bob Keane:

"I walked into the theater, it was a morning matinee for young people. The lights were up, and there was no stage actually. It was just in front of the screen. And here was this kind of a bull-like guy standing up there, a young fellow. And he was cranking away on a guitar with a little beat-up amp, and he was just really cookin'. It was terrific. Bo Diddley was one of

his big gods, and he had picked up a lot of stuff from him. It was that style, you know, really driving. I said, look at the way the audience is reacting, and he's really got something to say."

Keane introduced himself and invited Ritchie to lay down some informal demo tracks in his basement home studio. He found in Ritchie an undeniable talent, but also a very young man who hadn't honed his craft and lacked professional polish.

Bob Keane:

"Ritchie sat in a chair and started playing, and it soon appeared to me that he did not have one song completed all the way through. He was very unschooled and very raw. He knew three or four chords and everything he wrote was based on these chords. He had written some titles and words that he sang while he played, but he'd never written anything down. He'd make up songs and immediately forget them."

Ritchie returned to Keane's house the next few weekends to lay down tracks and solidify his song ideas. Ritchie had the unbridled energy of a teenager, and rock music was still in its infancy. Everything felt fresh and new, and Ritchie's talent flourished quickly. He signed on with Del-Fi in May of 1958—since he was still a minor, his mother had to sign the contract.

Ritchie Valenzuela might not have known it, but his brash dreams were about to come true—and very quickly. There was one matter to attend to, though, before his first record would be released.

Bob Keane:

"Music was very segregated back in '58. Black was black, brown was brown, blues was blues. And each one had its little niche. And if it was Latin, and if it wasn't a star or something from South America or Mexico, it was in the wastebasket. So I figured if we ship this record out with Valenzuela on it, you're never gonna get any airplay. So that's why I cut it down to Ritchie Valens. Ritchie didn't really object at all and neither did his family. They kind of put it in my hands, although he did have a loyalty to his culture."

— *Jiles Perry Richardson, ten years old.* —

Ritchie Valenzuela had become Ritchie Valens, the name by which he would hence forth always be known. He went into the studio and recorded "Come On, Let's Go," a raucous original, backed by a sly-humored cover of "Framed," a tongue-in-cheek Jerry Leiber/Mike Stoller number that had been a hit for the R&B group the Robins. The recording took place on July 8, 1958, in Studio B of Hollywood's soon-to-be legendary Gold Star Studio.

It's difficult today to imagine how quickly a star could be made in the early days of rock 'n' roll. Today a hit takes a concerted effort of promotion, publicity, image, radio, video, and luck. In rock's infancy, a record could be cut and released within days. Young people were hungry for this new music that evoked raw energy and sexuality, and an unknown could become a star within days or weeks of laying down a track in the studio.

This is what was about to happen to Ritchie Valens. His rise to stardom was nothing short of meteoric.

A week earlier, a Texas disk jockey named J. P. Richardson had also entered the recording studio armed with an original composition. He was about to become another overnight sensation.

Jiles Perry Richardson was born October 24, 1930, in Sabine Pass, Texas. He was the oldest of a Texas oil-field worker's three sons. The Richardson family subsequently moved to Beaumont. They were close-knit but poor. Like Ritchie Valens, a disadvantaged youth would motivate J. P. with a deep-seated desire to make money, succeed, and provide for those he loved and cared about.

J. P. had a quick wit, and a gift for gab that showed itself early in life. He started working part-time at KTRM radio in Beaumont while he was in college. He studied law for a while at Lamar College while still working at the radio station. In 1952, twenty-one-year-old J. P. married Adriane Joy Fryou, nicknamed Teetsie, who gave birth to a daughter, Debra Joy, in 1954. J. P. did a two-year stint in the army as a radar instructor, then returned to KTRM after his discharge.

Jerry Boynton:

"J. P. and I met through the radio business. I went to work at KTRM in Beaumont because I needed a job, frankly. I was a part-time announcer and I entered the business at seventeen. He was twenty-two at the time. [When he] went into the army and came out he was a changed man, because he was determined that he needed to make money to support his family . . . I think that J. P. was worried about being able to effectively take care of his family. He wanted his family, as many of us do, to have better than he had as a youngster. And he tried his best to do everything he could to make that happen."

J. P. was hard-working and ambitious. He cooked up an idea for a discathon; J. P. would stay awake at the station and play records for as long as he could hold up. J. P. set a record by staying awake and on the air for 122 hours and eight minutes—just more than five days. It was a popular move, but one that could have endangered J. P.'s health.

Jerry Boynton:

"The discathon was an idea that he had which was very popular in Beaumont. The people came from miles around to see this man try to stay awake. About day three that he had been awake, he looked terrible. He said, 'Jer, you think I'm going to die?' And I said, 'J. P., I think you are.' [laughs] I was really concerned about him. I took him upstairs in an elevator and refreshed

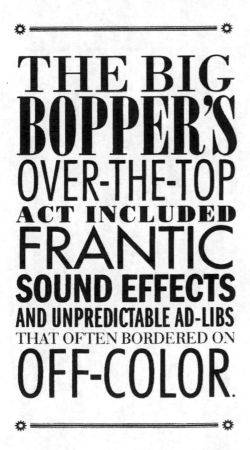

him a little bit. We came back down and he went back to work and made it. Of course when the discathon ended, he was hauled out to an ambulance. I don't recall how many days he was awake, but it was plenty. He would try almost anything like that to further his career."

J. P. served as program director at KTRM while doing as many as three on-air shifts a day. The exposure made him a popular local personality—or, perhaps more accurately, *two* personalities. In the morning he was the laid-back J. P. Richardson. But on his late-afternoon show, he transformed into the jivey, hyperactive Big Bopper.

The Big Bopper's over-the-top act included frantic sound effects and unpredictable ad-libs that often bordered on off-color. He was an improviser and a quick thinker, and he somehow managed to convey a knowing nod and wink through the speaker of the radio. He became a popular pitchman for products that he advertised on the air. He also borrowed African-American slang, an unusual and potentially risky move in the conservative climate of '50s Texas.

Jerry Boynton:

"A lot of people thought he was black. A lot of black people thought he was black. To him, it wasn't a racial thing at all. He wasn't trying to be one or the other. The Big Bopper was an identity unto itself. He was accepted by all races equally, I can assure you of that."

The Big Bopper mined a side of J. P.'s personality that others had only glimpsed. J. P. was outgoing and friendly, but the Bopper was another thing entirely.

Jerry Boynton:

"When the Big Bopper first hit the airwaves, J. P. Richardson would turn off all the lights in the studio and would stand up to do this

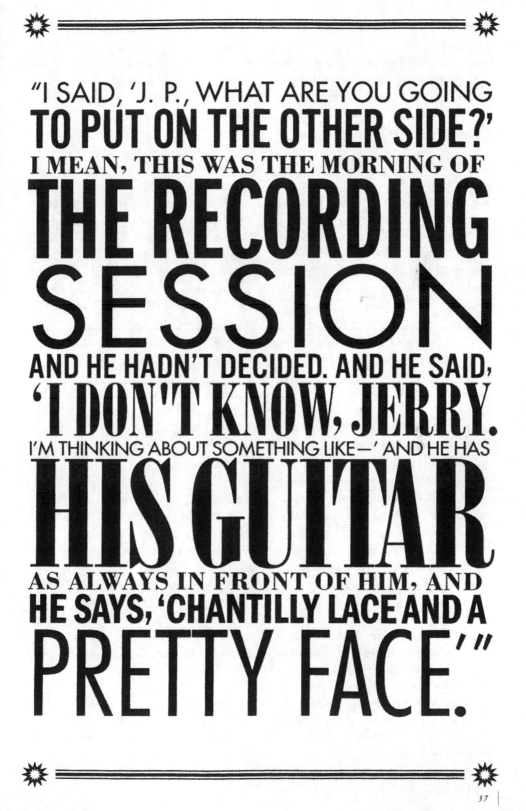

"I SAID, 'J. P., WHAT ARE YOU GOING TO PUT ON THE OTHER SIDE?' I MEAN, THIS WAS THE MORNING OF THE RECORDING SESSION AND HE HADN'T DECIDED. AND HE SAID, 'I DON'T KNOW, JERRY. I'M THINKING ABOUT SOMETHING LIKE—' AND HE HAS HIS GUITAR AS ALWAYS IN FRONT OF HIM, AND HE SAYS, 'CHANTILLY LACE AND A PRETTY FACE.'"

program. He never sat down, because he had to have all his energy that he could muster to perform as the Big Bopper. He would stomp and clap his hands, and do all these movements and motion. This whole atmosphere inside that studio that he was in—it was a small studio, but it was electric. You could feel it."

J. P. was no fool; he saw the rock 'n' roll explosion from the sidelines of his DJ studio and realized that fortunes were being made. He was older than most of the kids who made and listened to the music, but he dabbled in songwriting in his spare time and began to view music as a possible route to financial security for his family. It helped that he had a genuine love for rock music, and got a charge from writing songs. At first he viewed himself as a songwriter rather than a performer, but those around him knew that the Bopper persona had an appeal that could go places J. P. might not travel on his own.

Jay P. Richardson (the Big Bopper's son): "He worked in radio, and it didn't pay that great. That's basically the reason he went into the music business. He would have preferred to stay home if he could have made a couple of hundred bucks a week in radio. So that's when he took his character in radio and took it to the music. [It] just kind of went from there . . . he obviously was very talented in radio. [He] knew how to sell himself. I just think he was very talented."

J. P. wasn't an accomplished musician, but he had an intuitive sense for music. Between shifts he would go into a darkened studio, play guitar, and compose music for hours. Through an acquaintance, J. P. got a deal with Mercury Records and released a pair of straight country-and-western singles under his nickname "Jape" Richardson. Neither release stirred up much interest.

Maybe his entry into the music world, J. P. realized, wasn't going to come as a straight performer. As a DJ he was in the trenches of the music world. He saw first-hand what was popular, and he knew what the kids were requesting. One form of music that was getting a lot of attention was the comedic novelty single. J. P. put two and two together. He knew he was funny. He also knew that the Big Bopper was a lot funnier.

Jape the songwriter shook hands with the Big Bopper. It was a perfect match.

Two hits of the day were Sheb Wooley's "Purple People Eater" and David Seville's "Witch Doctor." J. P. combined the two and came up with "The Purple People Eater Meets the Witch-Doctor." He needed a flip side, so he hastily recorded a humorous rock number with a cheerfully lascivious phone monologue that he largely improvised in the studio. The song was called "Chantilly Lace."

On June 30, 1958, Jerry Boynton drove his friend to Houston to cut the single. He also provided a chirpy, sped-up voice for the A-side.

Jerry Boynton:
"I picked him up at his apartment. I said, 'J. P., what are you going to put on the other side?' I mean, this was the morning of the recording session and he hadn't decided. And he said, 'I don't know, Jerry. I'm thinking about something like—' And he has his guitar as always in front of him, and he says, 'Chantilly lace and a pretty face.' We went through that a little bit, and he was creating this the morning of the session. He said, 'I'm going to be on the telephone, I'm going to be talking to this chick, and I'm just going to wing it.' "

The single was released regionally on "Pappy" Dailey's D label. Dailey then convinced his bosses at Mercury to give J. P. another shot and release the record nationally. The manic

"Purple People Eater Meets the Witch-Doctor" flopped. But then disk jockeys flipped over the record. "Chantilly Lace" was all bluster and swagger. It had a squawking saxophone and an infectious chorus. The little number that J. P. recorded off the cuff was about to make him one of the biggest stars in rock.

Buddy Holly's fortunes were also taking him from obscurity to greatness. His country singles with Decca were failures. The company released "Blue Days, Black Nights," which previewed Buddy's rockabilly style and the vocal hiccup that would become one of his trademarks. Decca promoted the single half-heartedly, seemingly unsure whether it was country or rock 'n' roll.

Owen Bradley (producer, from John Goldrosen's *Remembering Buddy*):
"Paul said he wanted it country—at least, that was my understanding—and it was my job to please Paul Cohen. . . . Our musicians were fantastic at what they were doing, but they just didn't know how to do what *he* was doing. Buddy was trying to make sort of a rock 'n' roll record, and he should have had guys with a black feel. Our guys had a country feel. . . . I think we gave him the best shot we knew how to give him, but it just wasn't the right combination, the chemistry wasn't right. We didn't understand, and he didn't know how to tell us."

Buddy and his new band called themselves the Two-Tones, although Decca insisted on billing them as the Three Tunes. Although Buddy's single went nowhere nationally, he did win spots on a pair of fairly high-profile country package tours of the Southwest. Buddy tried, unsuccessfully, to perform without the eyeglasses that he'd worn since high school. He tried contact lenses, but found them uncomfortable and abandoned the idea after losing a lens on stage. Another time he took the stage without glasses or lenses; he dropped his guitar pick and had to crawl on his hands and knees to find it. The glasses were staying.

Travis Holley:

"He said, 'I might not have the looks but I got more talent than they've got.' I think he was a little self-conscious about [his image]. Nearly everybody raised back in those days in this part of the country, there's hard water here gives a brown stain on your teeth. Well the first thing he had to do was get his teeth capped. He tried contact lenses for a while but they didn't seem to work. And I think later on (record producer) Norman Petty told him, 'Well, you're you. You're just going to have to be you and wear glasses, and that's all there is to it.' It didn't seem to make much difference after that."

Buddy was trying to get his rock 'n' roll image together, but his first attempt at recording was a bust. Buddy's contract with Decca was terminated in January of 1957. No one was surprised.

Another option presented itself. He drove to Clovis, New Mexico—just over the Texas border—and met with producer Norman Petty. Petty owned and operated a well-regarded recording studio that bore his name. Buddy had cut demos there earlier, and had even considered trying to talk Decca into letting him record at Petty's studio instead of Owen Bradley's. Now Buddy thought that maybe his first instinct had been right all along.

Petty wasn't thirty yet, but he was already a seasoned veteran. He would be vital to Buddy's success, but he was no rock 'n' roller. His own tastes ran to the cocktail jazz he performed with his group, the Norman Petty Trio. They had scored a minor hit with a version of Duke Ellington's "Mood Indigo" in 1954; the money he made from the single had enabled Petty to build his studio. Petty had been frustrated by the hourly rates charged by typical studios, and had a different policy: He charged by the session.

Bill Griggs:

"Buddy went to see Norman Petty in early '57 over in Clovis. Norman Petty always said, 'Creativity doesn't come by the hour.' So whether you're in there two hours for one song, or twelve hours, it cost you the same amount of money. So you could be creative, you could do what you want, you could experiment and do new things. Buddy met with Norman Petty, Norman said, 'Write some new songs and come back.' And he went back on February 25, 1957, cut a song called 'I'm Looking for Someone to Love.' That was the A-side, on the B-side was a remake of a song that he had done in 1956 in Nashville called 'That'll Be the Day.'"

Buddy thought he might be on to something. He recorded a new composition and backed it with a rocking new version of a song

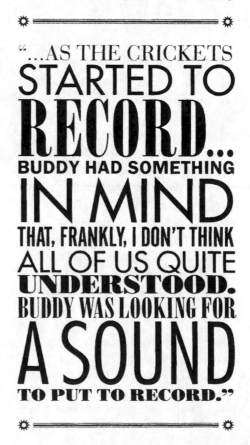

"...AS THE CRICKETS STARTED TO RECORD... BUDDY HAD SOMETHING IN MIND THAT, FRANKLY, I DON'T THINK ALL OF US QUITE UNDERSTOOD. BUDDY WAS LOOKING FOR A SOUND TO PUT TO RECORD."

he'd recorded in his failed Nashville sessions. Working in Petty's studio lent Buddy invaluable time to find his sound, and an atmosphere in which he began to learn about the technical specifics of the recording process. Some would later say that the world of Petty's studio had another side—represented by the fact that Petty tended to take control for himself of the potentially valuable publishing rights of the songs he produced for the artists who recorded at his studio.

British author Philip Norman, in his extensively researched Holly biography *Rave On*, paints a complex portrait of Petty. Norman depicts Petty as technically proficient but creatively mediocre. Petty had an air of piety—he abhorred alcohol and cigarettes, always kept a Bible on hand in the studio, and was prone to quoting Scripture in everyday conversation—that may have masked a repressed, secretive, controlling personality.

Whatever was the case, look at the songwriting credits on old records from the '50s. Many songs were composed by professional songwriters, but songs composed by the actual artists tend to have other names attached to the credits. These other names run the gamut from producers to managers to impresarios—their names added to the label meant money for them, and was a way of ensuring they benefited from the stars' success.

Business was business. Still is. No one can deny the pivotal role of Norman Petty in Buddy Holly's story. What's more, some feel that painting a revised picture of Petty in retrospect is unfair.

Bill Griggs:

"Norman Petty has been accused in books and things in later years, after his death, of ripping off the group, of taking money that he hadn't earned. I can't find proof of that. He took every dime coming to him as manager, 10 percent, he took his publishing money,

which is 50 percent, but that's all legitimate. He's gotten a bad rap through the years, I believe. Norman Petty was a man with a golden ear. This man was a great engineer in the studio, he knew what made a good sound. He didn't like rock 'n' roll, but he knew what was good, and he knew when Buddy Holly and the Crickets came and did 'That'll Be the Day' that he had something going."

Holly took a new band into the studio to cut his tracks with Petty. Jerry Allison played drums. Old bandmate Larry Welborn sat in on bass, and Buddy brought in nineteen-year-old former schoolmate Niki Sullivan on guitar. Niki was lanky and wore glasses, and could have passed for Buddy's brother. In fact they were actually distant cousins, a fact they wouldn't learn about until several months later.

Niki Sullivan:

"Buddy was always the leader in our group. Buddy had the experience. He had already done touring with country shows and had done recordings on Decca Records. Though he was young he still knew his way around a little bit. But as the Crickets started to record or practice more together Buddy had something in mind that, frankly, I don't think all of us quite understood. Buddy was looking for a sound to put to record."

While he waited to see whether this new phase of his recording career would pan out, he helped out at his brother Larry's company, Holley Tile. Sometimes he laid tile. More often he spent his working hours singing, strumming, and beating out rhythm on boxes of tile.

Larry Holley (*Texas Monthly*, 1995):
"Nah, Buddy didn't do a lot of work, but I didn't mind. I just loved to hear him play."

When Buddy hit the studio with Norman Petty and his new band, he brought his steely resolve and his sense of purpose to the tracks they recorded. The bulk of studio time was spent on "I'm Looking for Someone to Love"; "That'll Be the Day" was knocked out in four takes.

In return for his production services, the use of his studio, and his industry connections to find a record deal, Norman Petty took control of the songs' publishing rights. He also added his name to the songwriting credits—despite the fact that Buddy had written the A-side alone and written the B-side with Jerry Allison. This is how it was done. Petty argued that he was devoting his time and services for no money up front, which must have seemed more than reasonable to Buddy, who wanted his songs to be heard.

The fact that Buddy had already recorded "That'll Be the Day" for Decca caused complications, even though the label never released the song and didn't intend to. Buddy had signed a contract with Decca, and his use of the songs he recorded in Nashville was limited. Petty theorized that if the song was released under a group name Decca might not catch on. They needed a name. Buddy suggested "the Beetles," but Allison objected. They finally settled on the Crickets.

The Crickets found a permanent bass player in sixteen-year-old Lubbock native Joe B. Mauldin. They continued to rehearse, and a new sound started to emerge.

Niki Sullivan:
"A lot of people tried to put a handle on [the Crickets's sound]. We were not necessarily rhythm-and-blues. We loved it and we played it, but we were not a rhythm-and-blues band. But we weren't country either. We weren't rock 'n' roll either. We didn't know what we were, but we didn't sit around worrying about it. We just did our thing and people liked it."

Clovis was so far away from the music-business hubs of New York, Nashville, and Los Angeles, that it might as well have been on the moon. But Petty, unlike a lot of independent producers, was well connected. He had ties to Columbia Records and the powerful music publishing firm Peer-Southern music. Unfortunately, Columbia at the time had a strict anti-rock policy.

But Peer-Southern general manager Murray Deutch heard "That'll Be the Day" and knew it could be a hit. He agreed to help Petty shop the record—in return for half the publishing rights to both songs. Deutch found a receptive ear in Coral Records's Bob Thiele, a noted jazz producer. Thiele had reservations—his label had recently tried and failed to break the Johnny Burnette Trio, its only rock act. Another strike was that Coral Records's executives felt Buddy's raucous song might tarnish their label's image. A deal was struck, and three weeks after the first Clovis sessions the Crickets were signed to Brunswick, a Coral imprint. The label paid a hundred dollars for the master recordings, and pressed 1000 copies.

The Brunswick contract was signed by Allison, Sullivan, and Mauldin—who hadn't even played on the record. Petty was still trying to keep Buddy's involvement a secret from Thiele and Decca. It didn't work. Coral Records was, in fact, a subsidiary of Decca. But Decca got wind of Buddy's involvement with the Crickets and threatened to sue. Buddy had to waive future artist royalties from the Nashville version of "That'll Be the Day."

Brunswick released the single. It failed to stir up much interest at first, and it would take more than two months to enter the *Billboard* charts.

Then something happened. *The Buddy Holly Story* depicts a DJ in Buffalo locking himself in his studio and playing the song nonstop. The truth is that a DJ from Buffalo's WGR began programming "That'll Be the Day" three or four

times an hour. A DJ at the influential Philadelphia station WDAS started playing the song frequently for its African-American audience, spurring Decca to step up its promotion. The single broke out in a series of regional markets, then reached number one on the pop chart.

Travis Holley:
"I believe that when 'That'll Be the Day' came out that we realized we had a superstar on our hands. Until then we figured he might be somebody that just puts out a few records and sells a few, and might be able to make a pretty good living playing at dances and such. But 'That'll Be the Day' came out, which was his first smash hit, you know, and we knew—'Uh-oh, he's gone.' And he was."

Brunswick's single credited the song to the Crickets. They decided to also release records under Holly's name, hoping that the perception of two separate recording entities would generate twice as much money, airplay, and hits. Few in the business were convinced that rock was going to last more than a few more months, and putting Buddy in the public eye might have been a strategy for eventually moving him into a career as a more "grown-up" pop artist once the rock fad died out.

Buddy signed a separate contract with Coral, although records issued under his name would still feature the backing of the Crickets. No matter whose name was on the record, Buddy still insisted on splitting the money evenly with the Crickets—ignoring Petty's suggestion that the backing band be put on a salary.

When "That'll Be the Day" was taking off, Coral released Buddy's first official solo single on June 20, 1957. It was the swoony "Words of Love," with a distinctively unusual double-tracked lead vocal. Buddy was growing and

Travis Holley

experimenting at an astounding pace, and Norman Petty recognized it. At this point he became the Crickets's manager. Most seem to agree that Petty drifted into the job, with the band's encouragement. But by today's standards, Petty's wide-ranging role in Buddy's creative and business affairs might be considered fraught with conflicts of interest.

Everything was clicking. "That'll Be the Day" reached the Top 10 of *Billboard*'s R&B charts. The Crickets's surprise R&B success led to the band being mistakenly booked on an otherwise all-black bill for a tour of East Coast theaters with almost exclusively African-American audiences. The song's raw sound—along with the existence of an unrelated African-American vocal group called the Crickets—had led the booker to assume that he was hiring a black act. The Crickets played Baltimore's Royal Theater, Washington, D.C.'s Howard Theater, and a week-long run at New York's Apollo.

Niki Sullivan:
"From Baltimore we went to the Apollo in New York, and we did not know about the Apollo history. We just knew it was a date that we had to work, and we were going to work as hard as we could. They didn't know [the Crickets were white] until the curtains opened. Bear in mind

they've seen it all. What have you got for me lately? Nothing happened, and we went out for a second day and we didn't do very well. They did not like what we were doing at all. And it started to bother us. We were moved back to the worst position in the show, which was the break before the intermission. That bothered Buddy. But come the evening show, I'll tell you what—just before the curtains opened Buddy turned around and said 'To heck with it, we're going to open with "Bo Diddley."' The curtains open, Buddy steps up and cranks his guitar and we go right into 'Bo Diddley.' All of us, we had an event. We had a happening, because I was moving around on stage any way I knew how to do, Joe B. was doing the same thing on bass, and Jerry was working as hard as he ever worked on drums, and Buddy was knockin' 'em dead and the crowd went nuts. And we felt at home. This was great. Followed that up with a Little Richard song—the crowd went crazy. They found us, we found them."

"That'll Be the Day" was still number one on the pop charts on September 20 when Coral released a second solo single for Buddy called "Peggy Sue." It was a real original, with a ringing guitar, hiccupy vocal, and almost hypnotic drumbeat. The song was originally called "Cindy Lou" until Allison convinced Buddy to change the lyric in honor of Jerry's girlfriend Peggy Sue Gerron, whom he would marry the following year.

Peggy Sue Gerron:
"Buddy nor Jerry ever told me that they had written a song by the name of 'Cindy Lou.' Cindy was Buddy's niece, a brand-new niece that had been born. And Lou was his sister. And it had kind of a calypso beat. And they drove over to Clovis to record it, and it just didn't come off. And he started rewriting the song, and Jerry said, 'Well, let's put Peggy Sue's name on

there.' Because, at the time, I wasn't speaking to Jerry [laughs]. So I think Buddy was trying to kind of help the situation out. I love music, and he knew that. And so it's like he included me. It was just a gift."

"Peggy Sue" was an instant hit. It peaked at number three on *Billboard*. Buddy now had name recognition, and it was clear that his new releases had a built-in fan base. Buddy spent much of the latter part of 1957 on their biggest tour yet. It was an eighty-date package dubbed the Biggest Show of Stars for '57. The tour covered forty-three states and much of Canada. The bill included Chuck Berry, the Everly Brothers, Fats Domino, Eddie Cochran, the Drifters, Clyde McPhatter, Frankie Lymon and the Teenagers, and an orchestra that backed most of the acts—although not the self-contained Crickets. The performers traveled on cramped and noisy buses with the exceptions of Berry and Domino, who avoided the crush by taking their own cars.

Buddy struck up a friendship with the Everly Brothers. They were new on the scene but Buddy was impressed with their grooming and stagecraft. In turn, the Everlys admired Buddy's songwriting talents and the Crickets's self-contained lineup. The Everlys were dashing and cosmopolitan, and they were a big influence on Buddy's emerging sense of style. They introduced him to the world of classy restaurants and tailored clothes, and they talked him into trading his half-frame glasses for the black horn-rims that would become Buddy's trademark.

As for the Biggest Show of Stars, 96 of its 116 players were African-Americans. Buddy got to meet some of his idols, but the experience turned sour once the tour crossed the Mason-Dixon line. The Crickets had grown up in segregated Lubbock, but they were unprepared to see up close the virulence of Southern racism.

Niki Sullivan:

"[White artists] were indeed a minority and I can tell you right up front that it was a wonderful, down-to-earth, good home living experience. We were well accepted, they treated us like family. Traveling through the South, there were times when we could not all stay at the same hotel. We didn't understand it. There were restaurants where we could not share together. Restrooms, water fountains, it was strictly a divided society. That was very hard to accept, very hard to understand. Going into Louisiana the buses were stopped—two buses now, full of a hundred and fifty people. And they made all the blacks get on one bus and all the whites on the other. That was very, very crude and unfriendly, anything you want to say about it. But you did what you were told to do because the police were there. And they're enforcing the laws of their state."

On October 24, 1957, Brunswick released the second Crickets single, "Oh Boy." It was an aggressive track written by aspiring Texan rocker Sonny West (who would later become a member of Elvis's "Memphis Mafia" posse) and partner Bill Tilgman. The song was backed by the driving "Not Fade Away." On this song Jerry Allison wrote the song's sly surreal lyrics, and beat out a percolating Bo Diddley beat on cardboard boxes. In November the Crickets's debut LP, *The "Chirping" Crickets*, was released.

In December the band returned home from the road and played "That'll Be the Day" and "Peggy Sue" on *The Ed Sullivan Show*. They were reaching a nationwide audience. Sullivan's show had a huge following, and his reaction to the acts on his program could give them a huge boost. After the Crickets played, Sullivan called Buddy "Texas," shook his hand, and declared that the Crickets were nice boys. The imprint of Sullivan's approval was a massive boost.

Travis Holley:

"When he was on *The Ed Sullivan Show*, I believe that's the first time I saw him on television. We were all glued to it [laughs]. We thought he did a pretty good job. We were just bursting with pride. You know, once you make the Sullivan show, well, you're in. We thought he had made it, and of course he did."

Four days later, Niki Sullivan left the Crickets. He cited exhaustion as his reason for leaving, but his ongoing personality conflicts with Jerry Allison seem to have been a factor. The two had even come to blows in New York, leaving the drummer with a black eye that had to be airbrushed from the cover of their album. Regardless of the exact reasons, it was undeniable that the demands being placed on the Crickets were monumental. These were the costs of stardom.

Niki Sullivan:

"The grind, that you had to work twenty-one hours a day, and that had gone on for about five months. Something has to give and I gave. And I called back to the group and told them, that's it, I was disgusted with all of it and I was out of my mind from being tired and hungry. I wanted home cooking so bad. Those are the things that happened, and I don't regret quitting. That's too much work, too much to expect of people."

Buddy's momentum wasn't stopped. "Peggy Sue" and "Oh Boy" were in the Top 10 simultaneously. Buddy decided to continue the Crickets as a trio. The band made a hop to Honolulu, then went on to a week's worth of shows in Australia. Buddy's songs were topping the Australian charts, and the shows were a complete success.

In March 1958, Buddy's first solo album, *Buddy Holly* was released. The cover photo was a rarity, depicting Buddy without his glasses.

The band went on a three-month tour of one-nighters in Britain, where Buddy was already a hero. His records routinely charted even higher in the U.K. than back home.

Since Bill Haley had been the only other major American rocker to tour Britain, Buddy's appearances were a major event for British teenagers. After the Crickets played Philharmonic Hall in Liverpool, young Holly fanatics John Lennon and Paul McCartney avidly asked friends for detailed descriptions of the shows—it turns out the aspiring young musicians couldn't afford tickets. The pair loved Buddy's music so much that, when the time came for them to find a name for their group, they came up with the Beatles in honor of the Crickets.

The whirlwind of fame had caught up to Buddy Holly and the Crickets. There seemed to be no stopping them. After they returned to the States, they went back on the road on a six-week Alan Freed tour called the Big Beat Show. On their way home, Holly, Allison, and Mauldin stopped off in Dallas and bought three shiny new motorcycles. They made a triumphant return to Lubbock on their new wheels. Something else seemed to be going on as well, since the Crickets now felt comfortable making such major purchases on their own initiative, rather than getting approval first from Norman Petty. Petty still controlled the band's finances and produced them in the studio, but the trio of young men might already have been looking for a way out of Petty's control.

For the band's next Clovis session Buddy brought along guitarist Tommy Allsup, a twenty-six-year-old Oklahoman with a background in Western swing music. Buddy was so impressed by Allsup that he asked Tommy to play lead on "It's So Easy," a new composition. Allsup then played a Latin-inflected guitar part on "Heartbeat." Buddy decided that the Crickets would again be a foursome.

But as 1958 progressed, suddenly it seemed that while Buddy was growing in the studio, his creative strides weren't being matched on the charts. His solo single "Rave On" and the Crickets record "Think It Over" both suffered disappointing sales. Buddy went into a New York studio in June and cut the gospel-flavored "Early in the Morning." Declining sales weren't going to make Buddy retreat into formula; instead, he seemed ready to respond by making major changes in his life and art.

For a rock musician in the '50s, a couple of failed singles were the well-paved road to obscurity. Buddy was still famous, but suddenly he was no longer at the top. A few months went by, and suddenly his career was in transition. That was the way it worked.

Buddy seemed up to the challenge: He had ideas, he had the will. He was willing to change. Soon, though, he would need money. In order to make some cash, he would make a decision that would freeze his place forever in the history of the music.

FOR A ROCK MUSICIAN **IN THE '50s,** **A COUPLE OF FAILED** SINGLES WERE THE WELL-PAVED ROAD TO OBSCURITY. BUDDY WAS STILL FAMOUS, **BUT SUDDENLY HE WAS** NO LONGER AT THE TOP.

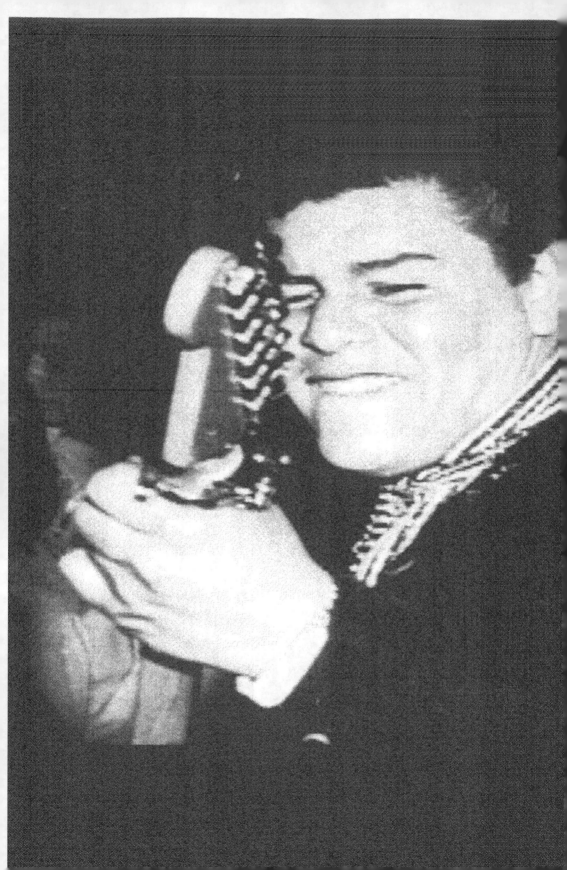

OH BOY!

At the moment Buddy Holly's career reached a sudden crossroads, Ritchie Valens was burning bright. "Come On, Let's Go" was released, and it was an instant local smash in Southern California. By September the song had entered the national Top 50. Valens was the first Mexican-American artist ever to cross over into the U.S. pop charts. The single went no higher than number forty-two nationally, but its impact was great.

> "MY GIRLFRIENDS AND I WERE **CRUISING THE DRAG ONE NIGHT...** AND ALL OF A SUDDEN THE DJ SAYS: 'RITCHIE VALENS'S NEW SONG.' IT JUST STARTED OUT WITH **'OH, DONNA,'** THE BEGINNING OF IT, AND ALL **MY GIRLFRIENDS STARTED** SCREAMING. WE HAD TO PULL OVER TO THE SIDE OF THE ROAD, I WAS SHAKING SO BAD."

Bob Keane:

"That damn thing just went *boom.* It was just incredible how fast that record went to number one here [in Southern California]. I went down to my distributor, and he gave me a check for thirty thousand dollars."

It was Keane's idea to follow up "Come On, Let's Go" with Ritchie's tender, romantic ballad "Donna." The teenage Ritchie Valens had started his latest composition as a tribute to his young love.

Donna Fox:

"He called me up on the telephone one night and said, 'I wrote a song for you.' That's all he said, he didn't say he was going to record it. And he said, 'Hold on, I'll play it for you.' So he strummed his guitar and started out with 'Oh, Donna . . . I had a girl, and Donna was her name.' And, of course I cried. He said, 'Did you like it?' And I said, 'Oh, it's beautiful.' "

The song Ritchie sang over the phone for Donna was probably substantially different from the one that he recorded with Bob Keane.

Bob Keane:

"Typically, Ritchie had only the title and the first line figured out: 'I've got a girl, and Donna is her name,' with no structure or meaningful lyrics to fill out the song. What he did was come to me with a four- or eight-bar riff, and I helped him rearrange the melody and its chord changes, and helped him write the guitar break . . . I just thought that he was really a balladeer. He had such a feeling when we got all through with it. I said, 'Boy, this has got a great sound.' And that's why we put it out. He really wanted me to do this song because he had written it for this girl, Donna."

Donna Fox:

"He mentioned nothing about it going to record, nothing. And my girlfriends and I were cruising the drag one night. There were four of us in my car. And all of a sudden the DJ says: 'Ritchie Valens's new song.' It just started out with 'Oh, Donna,' the beginning of it, and all my girlfriends started screaming. We had to pull over to the side of the road, I was shaking so bad. And I was trying to listen to it, but the girls were screaming and hollering, and I couldn't hear a darn thing. Anyway, in no time at all it was number one, and he called me up and said, 'We got gold, Donna, we got gold.' It was one of the most exciting moments of my life. What a compliment—to have someone write a song for you and for it to make him famous, more famous than he was."

Ritchie hit big with "Donna," which made all the girls swoon with its tender romanticism. But it was the single's adrenaline-driven Spanish-language flipside that made the kids rock. Ritchie had played a version of "La Bamba" for Keane while the two were driving in Keane's new Thunderbird from L.A. to San Francisco for Ritchie's first TV appearance. It was a seven-hour drive, and Ritchie sat in the backseat playing his guitar and singing every song he knew. One of the more obscure tunes that emerged from Ritchie's memory was "La Bamba." It was a traditional wedding song from Mexico. Ritchie had heard it in his childhood

and had been playing it live for years. But he didn't really know all the lyrics because of his limited knowledge of Spanish.

Bob Keane:
"It was very fast, you know. I said, 'Gee, that sounds like it would make a great rock record.' He said, 'Ah, no, I don't wanna do that.' When we got back I talked to his Aunt Ernestine. He didn't know the lyrics."

Ernestine Reyes (Ritchie's aunt):
"He came home and said that he had signed a record deal. I mean he was just jumping for joy."

Ernestine Reyes had supported Ritchie during his brief but meteoric career. Now she

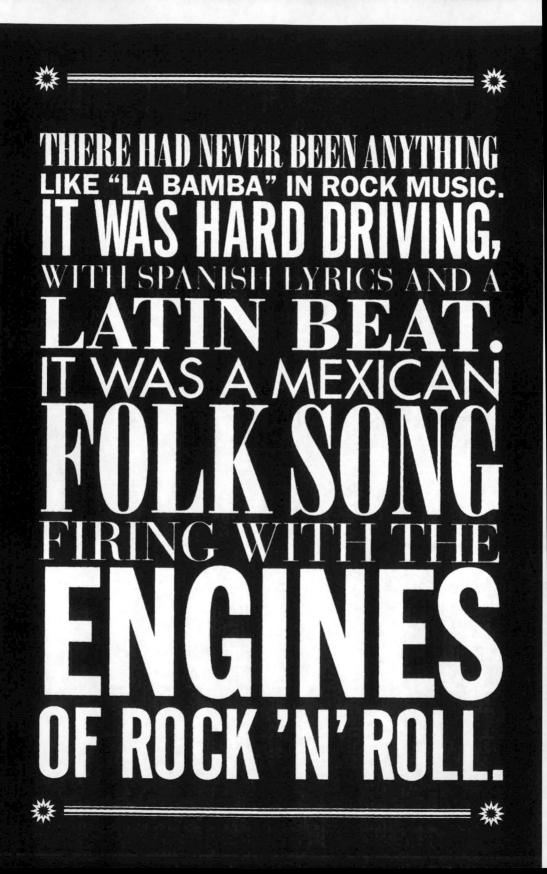

THERE HAD NEVER BEEN ANYTHING LIKE "LA BAMBA" IN ROCK MUSIC. IT WAS HARD DRIVING, WITH SPANISH LYRICS AND A LATIN BEAT. IT WAS A MEXICAN FOLK SONG FIRING WITH THE ENGINES OF ROCK 'N' ROLL.

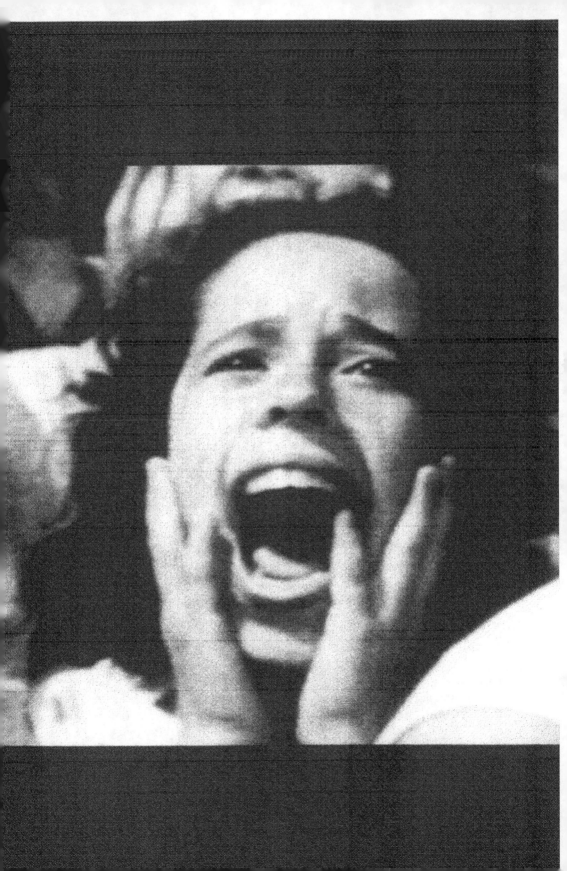

...HIS SUCCESS GRANTED HIM TO BE A HERO AT HOME. WITH KEANE'S HELP, RITCHIE USED HIS ROYALTIES TO MAKE A DREAM COME TRUE—HE BOUGHT A HOUSE FOR HIS MOTHER.

would help out Ritchie by providing him from memory with the lyrics to what would become his signature tune. Keane, who'd spent three years of his childhood in Mexico City while his contractor father helped build the Pan-American Highway, persisted when Ritchie initially felt that recording "La Bamba" would be exploiting his culture.

Bob Keane:
"'La Bamba' was first played in this hemisphere in the fourteenth century. 'La Bamba' comes from the word *mamamba,* which is the name of a native village in Africa. It was introduced by slaves who would chant the name of their village over and over because they were home-sick. A writer who told me that he'd researched

the origin of the song claims there's over 500 verses to it, and some of the verses don't make sense once they're translated. 'Yo no soy marinero, yo soy capitan.' That one means something like 'I am not a sailor, but I'm the captain.'"

There had never been anything like "La Bamba" in rock music. It was hard driving, with Spanish lyrics and a Latin beat. It was a Mexican folk song firing with the engines of rock 'n' roll. Like Ritchie, it was a specifically Chicano creation of Southern California. If the lyrics are hard to understand today, there may be good reason—Bob Keane says that Ritchie had so much trouble with the Spanish lyrics that Keane had to hold up cue cards in the studio.

Keane rush-released the double-sided single that paired "Donna" with "La Bamba." Some of L.A.'s top session musicians played on the tracks. The single came out in October of '58, and Ritchie was firmly established as one of rock's hottest new stars. "Donna" reached number two on the national charts, while "La Bamba" climbed to number twenty-two. The record was on the charts for three months.

Ritchie left his senior year at San Fernando High to focus on concerts and promotional appearances. A career in rock music was no sure thing—remember that many (if not most) Americans thought the music was nearing the end of its shelf life—so it was understood that Ritchie needed to capitalize on his sudden success. He set off on a series of gigs around California and the West Coast.

Ritchie's quick success made him a hero in Pacoima.

Gil Rocha:

"His house was like Grand Central Station. All his friends, and future friends, and former friends, and anybody who wanted to be his friend, just kept going to that house. And we all were happy, so excited, although some of them weren't so pleased about his changing his name. But it worked, so go with it. I mean, all of a sudden Ritchie's a star. What else could we ask for? It was the ultimate from our end of it, because other musicians were far away. Here our local hometown guy is doing it."

Surely more important to Ritchie was the opportunity his success granted him to be a hero at home. With Keane's help, Ritchie used his royalties to make a dream come true—he bought a house for his mother.

Connie Lemos:

"I can just remember thinking, 'No way. This is not going to be our house.' And they kept saying, 'Yeah, this is your house.' And we walked in and there were hardwood floors, and they were so shiny, and it was big. We had come from a one-bedroom home, very, very small, so it was probably three times what we were used to, and it was just so light and bright, it was just like a fairy tale. And Ritchie had actually bought it for mom."

Bob Keane:

"I had taken in enough money that I could put a down payment on a house for his mother before we went on tour. And that was the most important thing. He kept saying, 'I wanna get a house for my mother.' And I was so happy that we could do that for him, you know."

Ritchie finally was able to provide for the mother who had done so much for him all his life. And now it was time to hit the road and work.

Connie Lemos:

"All of a sudden, Ritchie wasn't there. My mom would tell us, 'Ritchie's making music, he's out there playing, and that's how he was able to buy us a house.' And then we'd turn on the radio and there would be Ritchie's music. We were all so proud. Bob Keane would bring pictures of Ritchie home for Ritchie to autograph. And, of course, we'd get into the pile before we went to school in the morning, and take pictures to school and sell them to the kids at five cents each."

Keane landed Ritchie an appearance in *Go Johnny Go*, the last of Alan Freed's rock 'n' roll movies. In the film, Ritchie performed "Ooh! My Head," lip-synching while strumming a guitar he's borrowed from Eddie Cochran. He also played a small part in a crowd scene during Chuck Berry's performance of "Little Queenie."

Ritchie spent most of the last three months of 1958 doing promotional shows. Ritchie and Keane flew east for a tour that hit eleven northeast cities in ten days—including choice spots on Dick Clark's *American Bandstand* and Alan Freed's TV show. In late November, Ritchie took a two-week working vacation to Hawaii. He performed at the Honolulu Civic Center along with Buddy Holly and the Crickets.

In order to go to Hawaii, Ritchie had to overcome the fear of flying that had plagued him ever since he witnessed the aftermath of the Pacoima crash during his childhood.

Bob Morales:

"When he went to Hawaii, he went to one of those machines at the airport where you buy the insurance. He went in there and got the maximum and then signed it and everything. And then he handed it to me and he says, 'Give this to my mom in case this sucker don't make it.'"

Connie Lemos:

"Flying was different back then that it is today. Us regular folk, we just got in a car or a bus or a train or whatever. For people in the fifties, flying was a big deal. Most people were afraid. I mean, you got into these little propeller planes, not like today."

Ritchie returned home safely on December 10 and played concerts at San Fernando High and Pacoima Junior High. The latter show was recorded and released after Ritchie's death, in 1960, as one of the first rock live albums, *Ritchie Valens In Concert at Pacoima Jr. High*. Ritchie was beginning to understand that being the front man of a rock band was hard work, but he possessed the energy and optimism of youth. Most of all, he was having a good time.

Later in December Ritchie flew again, this time to New York to play two weeks' worth of Alan Freed Christmas shows at New York's Loews State Theater. He played with the greats of the day, taking his place alongside Chuck Berry, the Everly Brothers, Frankie Avalon, the Moonglows, Jackie Wilson, and Eddie Cochran, who Ritchie had already become friends with when they shared stages in California. Ritchie showed off a flashy new mariachi-style outfit and appeared on several more TV shows.

Meanwhile, Bob Keane was working hard for his star client. He signed Ritchie with the booking agency General Artists Corporation. The first step in promoting Ritchie was landing him a spot on the Winter Dance Party, a three-week Midwestern tour beginning in late January. After the tour, Ritchie was to play four weeks in theaters on the East Coast. Plans for the immediate future included tours of Europe and Australia. Buddy Holly had proved that there was a global market for rock music, and Ritchie was going to be the next to cash in and spread his exposure.

On January 20, 1959, Ritchie went back to Gold Star and recorded three new tracks: "Stay Beside Me," "Hurry Up" (originally written by Eddie Cochran's girlfriend to memorialize the rocker's chronic tardiness), and "The Paddiwack Song," which was a rocking version of the nursery rhyme "The Children's Marching Song," otherwise known as "This Old Man."

That was it. It wasn't easy to lay down three tracks in a studio in one day, but Ritchie did it.

That night, Ritchie's mother threw her son a going-away party. Donna Ludwig wasn't allowed to go; her father forbade it.

Donna Fox:

"My mom smuggled me into the back room and said Ritchie was on the phone. So we talked for about a half hour, and he said this was a big trip, and that there were going to be a lot of stars. He was so excited about the stars that he was going to meet. I didn't get to go [to the party]. I was mad at my father for so very, very long. I didn't forgive him for that for a long, long time. Ritchie told me he would call me when he got home. And that was it."

Connie Lemos:

"It would have been just after Christmas that I sat up waiting for him, and then thinking, 'How come you have to go so fast again? You just got home.' He said, 'Oh, I'll be back. I'll be back.' He'd just gotten home, and here he was, leaving again. He was always excited about going out and playing his music. But I think he

was a little tired. As much as he wanted to do this, I think he missed being home, too. He was only seventeen."

Ritchie's aunt took him to the airport so he could fly east and begin the tour.

Ernestine Reyes:

"We took him that night and he was running a little late. You know, his song 'Hurry Up,' he really used to say that all the time. 'Hurry up, hurry up.' And I would always get insurance for him, and he says, 'I don't need that insurance, Tía.' I said, 'Yes you do, you're going to take it.' It only cost me a dollar or something. So he would go stand in line. And that was the last time we'd see him, when he left to Iowa on that tour."

The latter half of 1958 saw J. P. Richardson's fortunes rise at the same brief moment as Ritchie's. "Chantilly Lace" was an unexpected smash; it climbed to number six on the national pop charts and would eventually spend twenty-two weeks in the Top 40.

"Chantilly Lace" was the song that made everyone move their feet and instantly imitate the tune's opening "Helllllooooo baaaaabeeee!" The song climbed the charts and surprised everyone.

Jerry Boynton:

"'The Purple People Eater Meets the Witch-Doctor' was immediately forgotten and 'Chantilly Lace' was the rage. [J. P. was] absolutely, totally, unbelievably shocked. In the first place, J. P. was a humble person. So to have people flock around them the way they did, to hear more from this thing he had created called the Big Bopper, he was shocked. But quite pleasantly."

The Big Bopper was in demand for personal appearances and TV spots. J. P. had to go on and lip-synch his hit, which presented some problems because much of the song had been improvised off-the-cuff in the studio. J. P. knew this was his big chance. So he did what he had always done: rolled up his sleeves and worked as hard as he could.

Jerry Boynton:

"He had to practice over and over again the lip-synching because it wasn't set to rhythm. Talking on the telephone to this girl on the other end of the line wasn't set to any rhythm, it was just a person talking. So he and I spent many hours together practicing, I don't know how many hours we practiced together. It was a painstaking project to go through, but I think it came out quite well. J. P. wanted to be the best that he could be, and so he pressed himself very hard. I recall looking through the glass into the studio and perspiration was just rolling off him, you know, because he wanted to get it right."

J. P. worked up a stage act that played on the cartoonish aspect of the Big Bopper. He came up with outsized props and bulky, specially tailored suits that emphasized J. P.'s bulk. Suddenly this small-market DJ had a national persona and a way of making lots of extra money for his family. It was the chance of a lifetime.

The Big Bopper, though, was essentially a novelty act. J. P.'s friends and family remember him as an ambitious songwriter who might have parlayed his talent into a lasting career. But in the waning months of 1958, J. P. was compelled to push the Bopper as far as he could. He found out what many overnight sensations have learned: Nothing is harder than following up a debut smash. A pair of subsequent Big Bopper singles, "Little Red Riding Hood" and "The Big Bopper's Wedding," were only moderately successful. But J. P. knew that the public eye had yet to turn away from the Big Bopper, and he was determined to play as the Bopper until his time was over.

J. P. was going to make the most of his notoriety, and without a current hit this meant going on the road. Fellow Texan Buddy Holly recommended J. P. for a slot on the Winter Dance Party tour. J. P. jumped at the chance.

Jerry Boynton:
"When he started touring he had one daughter at the time. He didn't like to be away from his family. It was the hardest thing in the world for him, so he tried to stay in touch. He wrote his wife often. She didn't like it, but she felt the same way, frankly, that I did, which is that they needed the money and this was a way to get them ahead. But she really was very close to J. P., very devoted to J. P., and didn't like his being away."

After the Winter Dance Party, the Big Bopper was slated for an engagement in Las Vegas. This was alien territory for rockers, but it might have been an ideal showcase for a performer like J. P., who was able to entertain any kind of audience with his flamboyant, magnetic, riotous Bopper persona. J. P. had also accumulated twenty new songs that he hoped to either record himself or pass on to other artists. He'd started building a recording studio in his Beaumont home, and he and Jerry Boynton were looking into the possibility of investing in a radio station. J. P. was smart, and he had plans—plans that he put on hold when he took a leave of absence from KTRM and joined the Winter Dance Party.

Buddy Holly's life was undergoing big changes in the months before he joined the same tour. In June of 1958, he fell instantly in love with Maria Elena Santiago, a Puerto-Rican-born receptionist/secretary he met at Peer-Southern.

Travis Holley:
"Maria, his wife, has told me that he proposed

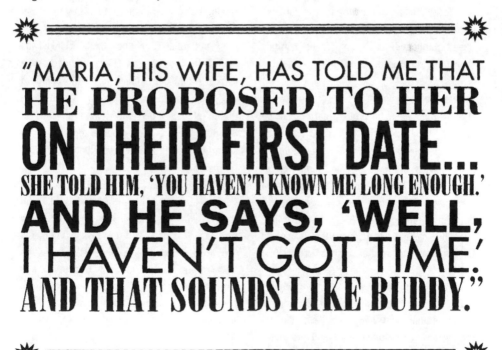

"MARIA, HIS WIFE, HAS TOLD ME THAT **HE PROPOSED TO HER ON THEIR FIRST DATE...** SHE TOLD HIM, 'YOU HAVEN'T KNOWN ME LONG ENOUGH.' **AND HE SAYS, 'WELL, I HAVEN'T GOT TIME.'** AND THAT SOUNDS LIKE BUDDY."

to her on their first date. I believe her, because Buddy was impetuous that way. She told him, 'You haven't known me long enough.' And he says, 'Well, I haven't got time.' And that sounds like Buddy. And I don't know whether he thought his life would be cut short, or his career would be cut short, but he was just in a hurry to do something, and he grew up in a hurry. He was more mature at twenty-two than I was at thirty. And that's about the only way I could explain it."

Buddy and Maria Elena were married on August 15 in a simple private ceremony at Buddy's parents' house. The couple honeymooned in Acapulco with fellow newlyweds Jerry and Peggy Sue Allison, who'd wed three weeks earlier.

Buddy's family, friends, and bandmates were happy for Buddy and charmed by his new wife. But things weren't going as well with Norman Petty. Petty warned that the marriage would spell doom for Buddy's appeal to his young female fans. In fact, the marriage wasn't publicized and didn't become widely known until after Buddy's death.

Travis Holley:
"I met Maria when he brought her here to be married. I had only heard about it a week before. Mother and Dad said, 'Well, Buddy's going to get married and he wants you to come.' I said, 'Well, yeah, I'll be glad to be there.' And when I met her, I understood why he wanted to marry her. She was just a little raven beauty. She was just as cute as she could be. And charming. And she still is."

But Buddy had been harboring doubts about Petty, and his contacts with others in the music industry led him to believe that his manager was unsophisticated and provincial. He and the Crickets grew increasingly resentful of Petty's control over their finances and the distribution of songwriting royalties. Buddy was a married man and a world-famous rock star; he resented having to go to Clovis with his hand out every time he needed some cash. Holly was always more interested in making music than making money, but he was irritated by the issue of the songwriting rights.

Waylon Jennings (the Crickets):
"Norman Petty never had him sign up with BMI or ASCAP, so he never got any performance fees for records. Norman got that. Buddy said, 'You need to take care of business and watch out, because they're not all good guys. They'll get you.'"

Buddy continued recording with Petty in the latter half of 1958. In September he brought renowned saxophonist King Curtis to Clovis to play on "Reminiscing" and "Come Back Baby." Curtis also played on a debut single Buddy was producing for his Lubbock pal Waylon Jennings.

That same week a new Crickets single was released: "It's So Easy." It's regarded as a classic today, but it failed to hit the *Billboard* Top 100. "Heartbeat," backed with "Well . . . All Right," placed little better when released in Buddy's name in November. Buddy began to separate himself from Norman Petty, going out on his own.

Buddy remained optimistic. He knew he had his talent, and he had learned a lot about the music business and the recording process. He moved to Greenwich Village in New York, instantly expanding his horizons. He was closer to the music business, and exposed to the energy and creative diversity of the city. He planned to launch his own publishing and recording company, Prism, which would function as an outlet for Buddy's talents as a writer, producer, and talent-spotter.

Buddy saw himself going over to the other side, from a performer to an industry player. The company was also to have roots in Lubbock, where Buddy wanted to build a recording studio—and where he saw himself returning after a few years spent setting up his business in New York.

Buddy initially convinced Jerry Allison and Joe B. Mauldin to join him in leaving Petty and relocating to New York. But it wasn't to be.

Peggy Sue Gerron:

"We looked at apartments in New York City and seriously considered moving. I think a big part of the fact that [Jerry] didn't want to live in New York was that in Lubbock he had the freedom of riding his motorcycle and running over to Norman's. You know, everything that had been neat in his life was in Lubbock, even though he loved performing and touring."

Home was home, and Jerry and Joe B. didn't want to leave theirs to follow Buddy's dreams. Norman Petty then talked the drummer and bass player into sticking with him and continuing to record as the Crickets without their leader. It was argued that the Crickets name had greater commercial value than Buddy's.

Buddy met with Petty in Clovis to sever their relationship. Buddy's one-time father-figure informed him that the Crickets were staying with Petty—and that he would be withholding Buddy's record and publishing royalties until all their disputes were resolved. Buddy was hurt and disappointed, but he agreed to let Jerry and Joe B. use the Crickets name.

Peggy Sue Gerron:

"The last meeting we had was at Busy Bee Cafe in Clovis. At that point, Buddy said, 'OK, then you take the Crickets name for a while and I'll go ahead and do my thing.' I don't think that would have lasted very long. I think Buddy wanted Jerry and Joe B. on the road with him, and I know that's where Jerry and Joe B. wanted to be."

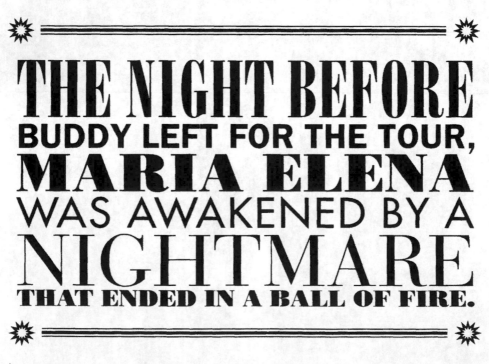

THE NIGHT BEFORE
BUDDY LEFT FOR THE TOUR,
MARIA ELENA
WAS AWAKENED BY A
NIGHTMARE
THAT ENDED IN A BALL OF FIRE.

Bill Griggs:

"There's been a lot of talk about why the Crickets broke up, and I don't think they like the word 'broke up.' They separated for a while because Buddy was going to live in New York at the time. Jerry and Joe B. decided they didn't want to go to the big city. So they separated, and according to everybody I've talked to, it was very amicable. If anybody wanted to get back with Buddy, all he had to do was give him a phone call."

There was no denying, though, how major a change this represented for Buddy. Suddenly he was without his backing group and two friends, he was without the Crickets name, and he was without the manager and producer who had helped shape his career to date. Although he was exhilarated by the possibilities, cutting ties with Norman Petty represented a giant leap into the unknown.

Bill Griggs:

"I think one of the reasons that Buddy left Norman Petty was Buddy wanted to manage himself. He really wanted to push, push, push, and attain all these very high goals he had set for himself. I think he wanted total control of his music from writing a song all the way out to owning a pressing company at one time to press the records. He would have owned everything lock, stock, and barrel. That's probably one of the reasons he got away from Norman. I can tell you this, on the business cards for Prism Records, Norman Petty was listed on that card. I really don't think it was a bad split. I think Buddy just wanted to go out on his own, be his own boss. Everybody wants to do that."

Buddy returned to New York excited by his plans for the future. It seemed as though he was poised to become the first rock star to successfully step behind the scenes.

But there was a problem. The records hadn't been selling, and Buddy didn't have enough cash. Buddy's wife was pregnant now, and his royalties were still being frozen by Norman Petty. Buddy had planned to give up touring, at least for a while, to concentrate on his new business, but he needed some money right away.

Irving Field of the General Artists Corporation called up and offered Buddy a spot on the upcoming Winter Dance Party tour. Buddy accepted.

Bill Griggs:

"I think Buddy was very disappointed by that lull in [record sales]. And that's one of the reasons he took that tour. He was cash poor. But he also wanted to get out and show people that he's still around. He had a lot of holdings. He had publishing money due him and things like that. But he didn't have cash in his pocket. And the only tour he could have gone on was this Winter Dance Party tour."

The night before Buddy left for the tour, Maria Elena was awakened by a nightmare that ended in a ball of fire. She woke her husband, who said that he had just had a dream in which he, as a passenger in a small plane piloted by his brother Larry, had reluctantly flown off without her. The next day Buddy joined the tour.

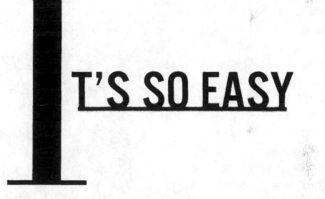

IT'S SO EASY

✸

The *Winter Dance Party was a three-week tour of one-night stands in the upper Midwest. As with other package tours common to rock 'n' roll's early years, multiple acts were expected to travel together between shows in crowded buses. The musicians earned their pay through enduring a grueling travel schedule and less than luxurious conditions.*

Many touring packages of the time were elaborate undertakings involving as many as twenty acts. The Winter Dance Party was more modest, featuring only five: Buddy; Ritchie; and the Bopper; along with New York up-and-comers Dion and the Belmonts; and Frankie Sardo, a little-known would-be heartthrob who warmed up the crowd as an opening act by performing renditions of other artists' current hits.

Buddy received a share of the tour's profits and a salary—compensation totaling about $3,000 to $3,500 a week, from which he paid his band. Ritchie and the Bopper received about $700 to $800 a week.

The acts on the tour were there for the pay and for the exposure. It was winter, and the Dance Party was the only major rock 'n' roll tour on the road that season. Whereas a more high-profile tour might have booked prestigious theaters in major cities, the Winter Dance Party focused on ballroom venues in smaller, out-of-the-way markets—many of which were rarely visited by major rock 'n' roll acts. One look at the tour's itinerary might have led any of the performers to wonder what he had gotten himself in for.

Bill Griggs:
"The Winter Dance Party was a major tour to those that went because it was in the upper Midwest. Thirty below zero, nothing's happening up there. So when a tour of that magnitude comes to town, it's a big deal. The problem was whoever scheduled the tour. They started way over here and went four hundred miles to the next venue, and then went back thirty miles from the first show for the next one. Hopscotching back and forth."

Tommy Allsup (Crickets):
"This was a tour that was going to take place in the middle of winter. It was cold, cold. I

don't know whose idea it was, but it was a really bad idea."

Crickets Jerry Allison and Joe B. Mauldin were still back in Lubbock, so Buddy had recruited three sidemen to serve as the Crickets—which is how they were billed, despite Buddy's agreement to grant his old bandmates control of the name. These new players were to double as a backup combo for the rest of the tour's acts.

Buddy's guitarist was Tommy Allsup, who'd already played on "It's So Easy" and "Heartbeat." On Allsup's recommendation, Buddy hired Texan Carl "Goose" Bunch to play drums. For bass, Buddy called on Waylon Jennings, an old Lubbock friend. Jennings's real

goal was to launch his own recording career, and Buddy had taken the deep-voiced singer/songwriter under his wing. Buddy advised Waylon on stage presentation and got him started in the recording studio.

Waylon Jennings:
"Buddy and I had been friends for quite a while. We went all the way back to when Buddy sang country music. I was a disk jockey at Lubbock, K-triple-L, and he came up there and

decided that we were gonna do this tour. He needed a band, so he'd gone downtown and bought a bass. He said, 'You've got two weeks to learn how to play that thing.' Well, I played guitar of sorts. Anyway, I memorized every one of his songs. I had no earthly idea what did what on a bass, but I memorized where to put my fingers for which songs. Which worked out good. About halfway through the tour, though, I realized the bass was the first four strings of the guitar, and I had to relearn everything then."

The Winter Dance Party coincided with the most severe winter in recent memory. The musicians endured bitter cold temperatures and dangerous road conditions from the start. They had to haul and set up their own stage gear. The musicians were packed together with their luggage and equipment into buses that traveled hundreds of miles through the night in raging snowstorms. Sometimes the temperatures would drop to thirty below zero. The situation was made even worse by the bargain-

basement charter company that was handling the tour. The tour's first bus broke down after a few hours. The second lasted a day.

Bill Griggs:

"They were reconditioned school buses, not good enough for schoolkids. Now picture that in your mind. It's not like the buses that stars have today, with VCRs and bedrooms and padded chairs and things like that. It's a rickety old school bus with very hard seats. The buses were falling apart, breaking down. They had five different buses on the tour before they drove into Clear Lake, Iowa. Every time a bus broke down, they replaced it with another rickety old bus. And that would break down in a day or two."

They were riding through brutal conditions, on a travel schedule that forced them to travel as much as 500 miles between shows in the dead of night. The schedule was so tight that there wasn't even time for laundry. The performers would leave the stage in their sweaty clothes and hit the bus. They did their best

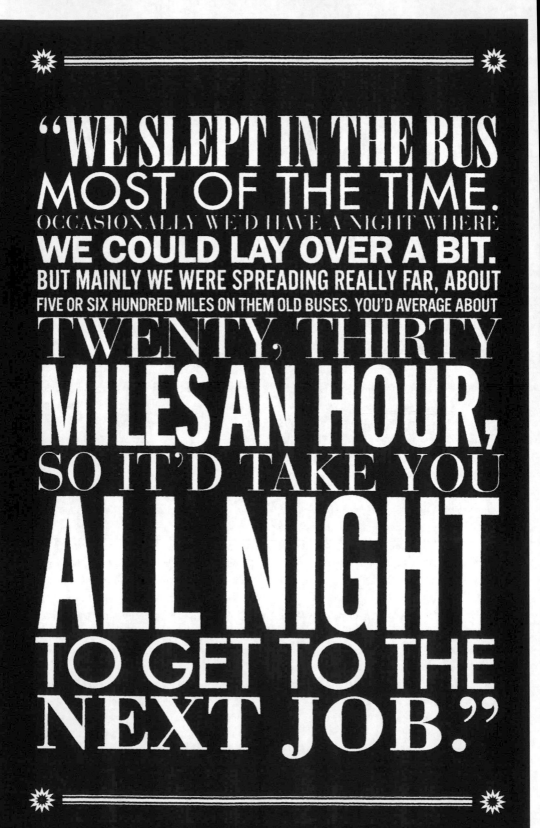

"WE SLEPT IN THE BUS MOST OF THE TIME. OCCASIONALLY WE'D HAVE A NIGHT WHERE WE COULD LAY OVER A BIT. BUT MAINLY WE WERE SPREADING REALLY FAR, ABOUT FIVE OR SIX HUNDRED MILES ON THEM OLD BUSES. YOU'D AVERAGE ABOUT TWENTY, THIRTY MILES AN HOUR, SO IT'D TAKE YOU ALL NIGHT TO GET TO THE NEXT JOB."

to catch some sleep in their seats, or in the overhead luggage racks.

Tommy Allsup:
"We slept in the bus most of the time. Occasionally we'd have a night where we could lay over a bit. But mainly we were spreading really far, about five or six hundred miles on them old buses. You'd average about twenty-five, thirty miles an hour, so it'd take you all night to get to the next job."

Waylon Jennings:
"I had no earthly idea. It was so glamorous in my mind before we went. Sometimes it was forty below. One of our buses froze up. We were cold all the time, and dirty most of the time. We would leave after one show sometimes and get [to the next one just] in time. What you do is

hold your breath from the time you left the bus until you got to the dressing room door. But we were in show biz. I got a lesson, a big lesson, from that whole thing."

The thermometer read twenty-five below zero on January 23, 1959, when the tour arrived at its first venue, the Million Dollar Ballroom in Milwaukee. It didn't get much warmer after that.

Still, as Waylon Jennings said, it was *show biz*. And the tour wasn't without bright spots. The harsh experience pulled the musicians closer together. And those who went to the shows say that the musicians were delivering spirited performances. The rockers played off each other, and camaraderie developed. Ritchie Valens, a long way from Southern California, tried to listen and learn.

Tommy Allsup:

"Ritchie was great. He was a good showman, and he played good rock 'n' roll guitar. He was only seventeen years old. When I was seventeen I was still learning how to walk, you know, but he was doing really good. We'd talk on the bus. He was very inquisitive, he asked a lot of questions. He asked Buddy a lot of questions. He was wanting to know how we set our amplifiers, what tones we used on our guitars, how we did this little lick. I guess he was trying to pick up things that we were doing, but he didn't need much coaching. He was on his way."

The tour proceeded. The shows could be euphoric, with roaring crowds of teenagers who had never seen rockers of such stature in their small-market towns. Then the lights turned off and the tour got onto another bus that limped its way through the black of night in the frozen heartland. After Milwaukee, this was the schedule that awaited the musicians on the Winter Dance Party:

Jan. 24: Eagle Ballroom, Kenosha, Wisconsin
Jan. 25: Kato Ballroom, Mankato, Minnesota
Jan. 26: Fournier Ballroom, Eau Claire, Wisconsin
Jan. 27: Fiesta Ballroom, Montevideo, Minnesota
Jan. 28: Prom Ballroom, St. Paul, Minnesota
Jan. 29: Capitol Theater, Davenport, Iowa
Jan. 30: Laramar Ballroom, Ft. Dodge, Iowa
Jan. 31: National Guard Armory, Duluth, Minnesota
Feb. 01: Cinderella Ballroom, Appleton, Wisconsin (cancelled)
Feb. 01: Riverside Ballroom, Green Bay, Wisconsin
Feb. 02: Surf Ballroom, Clear Lake, Iowa

Among the teenagers in the audience for the Duluth show was a devoted Buddy Holly fan

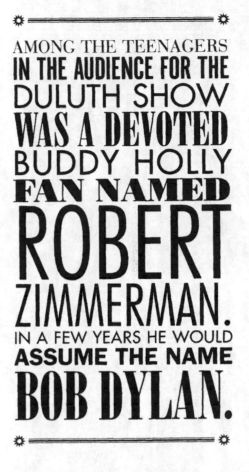

AMONG THE TEENAGERS IN THE AUDIENCE FOR THE DULUTH SHOW WAS A DEVOTED BUDDY HOLLY FAN NAMED ROBERT ZIMMERMAN. IN A FEW YEARS HE WOULD ASSUME THE NAME BOB DYLAN.

named Robert Zimmerman. In a few years he would assume the name Bob Dylan and make his own mark in the music business.

Buddy was the most experienced road warrior on the tour. He was still only twenty-two, but he assumed the role of elder statesman and father figure to many of the other musicians. He bonded with Ritchie, and was so impressed with the teenager's musical talent and unassuming attitude that he raised the possibility of Ritchie recording for his label—with Buddy in the producer's chair.

Waylon Jennings:

"Ritchie was just shy, you know. But what was wild was, he was wild on stage. It was like two different people. He was really quiet, and on

"RITCHIE WAS JUST SHY, YOU KNOW. BUT WHAT WAS WILD WAS, HE WAS WILD ON STAGE. IT WAS LIKE TWO DIFFERENT PEOPLE. HE WAS REALLY QUIET, AND ON THE BUS HE WOULD JUST KIND OF LOOK OUT THE WINDOW. HE'D LAUGH AT THE JOKES, BUT HE WOULDN'T TELL ONE. BUT WHEN HE GOT ON STAGE, HE WAS IN HIS ELEMENT AND THE ADRENALINE WOULD GET UP AND GOING. HE WAS A GREAT PERFORMER, HE REALLY WAS."

the bus he would just kind of look out the window. He'd laugh at the jokes, but he wouldn't tell one. But when he got on stage, he was in his element and the adrenaline would get up and going. He was a great performer, he really was."

Buddy missed Maria, who was pregnant. He called her twice a day from pay phones. He was also becoming preoccupied and upset by the increasingly complicated mess of legal and financial hassles related to his problems with Norman Petty. By most accounts, though, Buddy was in good spirits on the tour. He had a stomach condition that prevented him from drinking alcohol, including beer. The freezing temperatures made it impossible for him to honor his recent pledge to quit smoking. He was still enthusiastic about the music—and he was excited to discover that he could deliver a great performance without his former bandmates.

Tommy Allsup (to Philip Norman):
"Buddy wasn't uptight, he felt really good about being free of Norman Petty. He was always talking about the plans he had; the new studio . . . his European tour. He just seemed like he was about to explode."

Everyone on the tour was subject to the punishing schedule. It was soon apparent that there would be little time for laundering clothes or sleeping in a bed. A couple of hours in a hotel room washing up was quickly considered a luxury. And there was very little time for the sort of offstage carousing that rock 'n' roll tours are known for.

Waylon Jennings:
"We were pretty tame. I think about the most exciting thing on the whole tour was when Dion had this girl in the back of the bus. The next morning he was back there hollering, 'Don't nobody move, don't nobody move.' He had lost his contact lens. That's the first time I'd ever heard of a contact lens."

Tommy Allsup:
"Well, we'd sneak out at night and go drink a beer. Waylon and me, and the Big Bopper. We were really probably the only three guys old enough to get in a bar. You had to be twenty-one. And Buddy wasn't drinking beer."

One of the perils of the road the inexperienced young men quickly learned about was the enthusiasm of the young girls in their audience. It was still five years until Beatlemania, but rock 'n' roll was unleashing passions that had been pent up and repressed throughout countless adolescences.

Waylon Jennings:
"Girls were the hairy ones, let me tell you. They'd get a hold of you. I guess when they get excited, their strength gets so much. I mean, they'd grab you by the necktie and choke you to death. And they would get excited and rush the stage and what have you. But that was about all. Of course, sometime maybe you might have to fight with some old jealous boyfriend."

When the tour bus broke down on a remote section of Highway 51 outside Duluth, the musicians had to catch a ride into town, a few at a time, from passing motorists.

Tommy Allsup:
"I didn't realize that it got that cold, you know. Kids would be standing outside those places and it would be twenty-five below zero. [The tour] was pretty reckless. I don't know where they got them old buses, but they were worn out. The heaters wouldn't work on them. One was going down the highway, we'd played Duluth, Minnesota, and were on our way to

Green Bay. The bus was going up this kind of little hill, and the bus just stopped, just froze. And there we sat, in a snowstorm with the bus frozen. That's the night our drummer's feet got frostbite. We were burning papers in the aisle, trying to stay warm."

Carl Bunch suffered frostbite on his feet and had to be hospitalized for several days. The musicians made it to the next gig by train and Greyhound bus while they waited for another restored school bus to be dispatched.

The tour made the stop in Green Bay. Ironically, it was cited by some as the best of the tour. Dion and the Belmonts bass singer Carlo Mastrangelo sat in on drums for most of the night, taking Carl Bunch's place. Ritchie took over the drum kit for the Belmonts's show.

Such moments fostered the solidarity among the musicians. They all understood that there is often no better place for creative sparks to emerge than the close quarters of the road. They also understood the flip side—that the road can be a deadening trial.

Bob Keane:
"I called Ritchie on the pay phone and got him. He was telling me some of the problems they were having. The bus was breaking down and people were freezing their feet. The reason he didn't come back right away was because he felt that his fans had paid their money and it was his obligation to appear. I said, 'Look, Ritchie, shine it. Get on a train and I'll send you the money. Just get going.' He said, 'Well, OK.' I thought he was gonna come home."

The Winter Dance Party had an open date on February 2, and at the last minute a gig was booked in Clear Lake, Iowa, at the Surf Ballroom. Getting there required an even longer drive than usual. The musicians were riding in their sixth bus in ten days, and it was a 350-mile trip from Green Bay to Clear Lake. Midway, they had to stop to get the heaters fixed.

J. P. Richardson was battling the flu with a concoction of whiskey and mouthwash. He was in a state of continual discomfort, and squeezing his physical bulk into the cramped confines of the bus wasn't making things better. He took advantage of a stop to buy a sleeping bag at an army surplus store, hoping that it might help him get comfortable for the next all-night ride. Meanwhile, Buddy was on the phone to his lawyer in New York. The lawyer said that, despite the threat of legal action, Norman Petty was still refusing to free up Buddy's royalties. The news didn't do much for Buddy's morale.

Tommy Allsup (to Philip Norman):
"When he got back on board the bus, he was really upset. He said, 'When this tour's over, I'm going back to Clovis and I'm going to kick Norman Petty's ass. I'm going to get my money out of that studio, one way or the other.'"

The bus pulled into the Surf Ballroom parking lot at around six—just two hours before showtime and too late for the performers to make a scheduled 4:30 personal appearance at a record store in nearby Mason City.

Clear Lake is about 200 miles north of Des Moines and 150 miles south of Minneapolis. The Surf Ballroom got its name from its beach decor, which was quite a contrast to the countless miles of farms and cornfields outside. It was rare for major touring acts to visit Clear Lake, so for the Winter Dance Party the ballroom moved its weekly rock 'n' roll night from Wednesday to Monday, and raised the admission price to $1.25.

When the touring musicians arrived, they were cold and exhausted. And they were looking for a way to ease the hardships they'd been forced to endure.

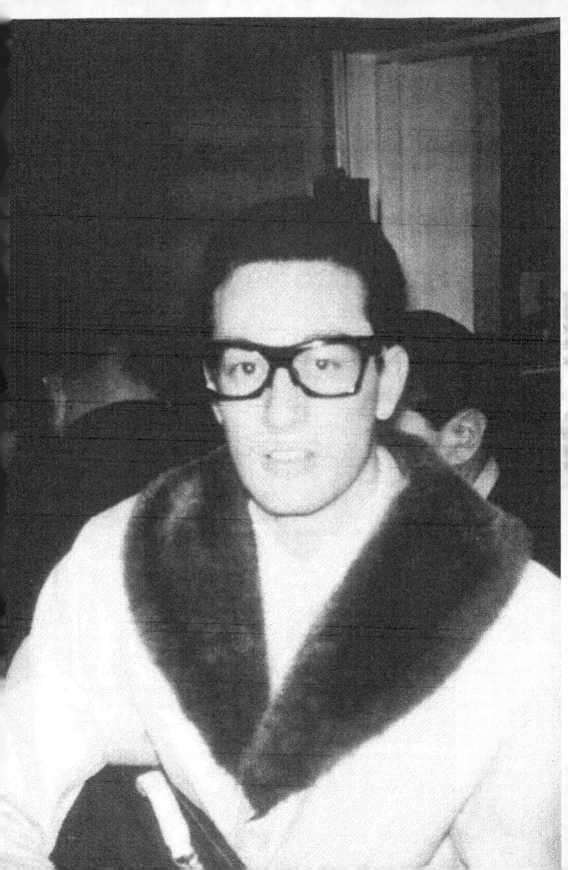

Carroll Anderson (manager, Surf Ballroom): "They were still jubilant young men. But they were very cold. They hadn't had any heaters for some number of hours. And they were thinking and planning ahead. They hadn't had a chance to get into a hotel room and have a good night's rest or get their clothing changed."

Buddy was exhausted and disgusted. He got the idea to charter a small plane to carry himself and his two remaining sidemen ahead to the next show at the National Guard Armory in Moorhead, Minnesota. It had been six days since any of them had enjoyed the luxury of a night in a hotel room.

Tommy Allsup:
"That was the reason Buddy wanted to fly, you know. So he could get some laundry done, 'cause we'd been out for twelve days and our shirts were starting to stand up on their own."

Waylon Jennings:
"I think they made a call from there and got a plane. It was a spur-of-the-moment thing."

Bob Hale was a disk jockey from local station KRIB. He usually served as the Master of Ceremonies for the Surf Ballroom's record hops, and he was enlisted to serve the same function for that night's show. Hale's wife was pregnant, like Buddy and J. P.'s, and they had dinner together before the show.

Bob Hale:
"While we were sitting there, J. P. Richardson said to my wife, 'Kathy, may I put my hand on your tummy?' She said sure. He said, 'This is what I miss most about being on the road, feeling my baby move in my wife's tummy.' And Buddy said, 'That's why I call Maria every day to see how the baby is doing.' Oh, boy, that hit us the next day."

The Winter Dance Party hit the Surf Ballroom stage before a full house of about 1,200 teens. The fans had braved cold weather, some traveling from as far as Illinois and Minnesota. When they weren't onstage, the stars greeted fans and signed autographs at a table to the side of the stage.

Carroll Anderson:
"Their type of rock music was a little different from what the locals were playing here. But as far as I was concerned it was better. A lot of the locals came out to see what was going on."

Waylon Jennings:
"It was a real up night. Everybody was rockin', everybody havin' a good time."

Frankie Sardo came on to loud applause and did his warm-up set. It was warm inside, with painted stars on the ceiling and the surf motif on the walls making the fans feel as though they had been transported someplace else, if only for the next couple of hours.

Bob Hale:
"In Mason City only we got Frankie Sardo up on the charts [laughs]. His record started to sell because the kids knew they were going to see

him. And so Frankie started the show. A very pleasant singer. He was very good."

Then the Big Bopper took the stage. He was wearing his trademark oversized zebra-skin jacket, ankle-length fur coat, and giant Stetson hat. J. P. was still sick with the flu and running a fever. He managed to sweat through his jacket while he was on stage, but he delivered a typically energetic set.

Bob Hale:
"The Big Bopper came out and did his telephone routine and had everybody laughing."

Bill Griggs:
"The most popular one on that tour was probably the Big Bopper, because when he came out and did 'Chantilly Lace' he really got the audience going and got them dancing and got them laughing and made them happy."

The atmosphere was growing more charged. The kids in Clear Lake had never seen stars of this magnitude, and now they were seeing three of the biggest stars of the day. Although Buddy was the tour's official headliner and biggest name, Ritchie's double-sided hit, "Donna"/"La Bamba," was tearing up the national charts. When he came out to play, he didn't disappoint the crowd.

Bob Hale:
"Oh my gosh the girls went crazy over Ritchie Valens. Young, good-looking Hispanic sexy-looking guy in that blue-green shimmering shirt of his. Ritchie Valens just owned that place. This was his first tour, never seen the United States before. So here he was in a foreign country called Iowa. He was about four seconds into his music and it was as if Ritchie had been there all his life. He had everybody singing and dancing to 'La Bamba,' and I don't know how many

times he had to sing that before we ended the first half of the show."

Because Buddy's drummer Charlie Bunch was still off the tour because of the frostbite he'd suffered on the bus, the musicians had to pitch in and help out. During Ritchie's set, fans in the audience might have been surprised to spot a familiar bespectacled face keeping time behind the kit.

Tommy Allsup:
"The show we did that night was kind of groovy because Ritchie played drums for Buddy, and Buddy played for Ritchie. Can you imagine Clint Black playing drums for Garth Brooks, and Garth playing drums for Clint—you know, another star? And I think about that, you know. Those guys were all right."

Buddy also sat in on drums for the Dion and the Belmonts set; he ducked the spotlight behind the cymbals. The Belmonts played their new, as-yet unreleased single, "A Teenager in Love," which would become a top five hit the coming spring.

Bob Hale:
"Dion and I made sure that the drums were set back of the stage and we put the lights off Buddy and put a hat on him. So at the end of the act I said to Dion, 'Introduce your group.' And he went around and I said, 'You forgot the drummer.' 'Oh, yeah,' he said. 'This is a young guy we had to pick up because Charlie Bunch is in the hospital. We call him Buddy Holly.' And with that, Buddy jumps up, grabs his guitar and sings 'Got to Travel On.' And then they switch sidemen."

Holly and his new Crickets played "That'll Be the Day," "Peggy Sue," "Maybe Baby," "Heartbeat," and "Rave On," along with rock standards such as Gene Vincent's "Be-Bop-A-Lula," Jerry Lee Lewis's "Whole Lotta Shakin' Goin' On," and for a finale, Chuck Berry's "Brown-Eyed Handsome Man."

While the stars were rocking on stage, Carroll Anderson was on the phone to the Dwyer Flying Service in Mason City. He was chartering the plane that Buddy had requested to carry three passengers to Fargo, North Dakota—the airport closest to Moorhead, Minnesota.

Carroll Anderson:

"I called to find out if it would be possible for them to leave at midnight out of here. I went back to Buddy right before he went on stage and told him that it was a hundred and six or a hundred and eight dollars, but that was for three people."

That night, a lonely, tired Ritchie was also on the phone—to his brother Bob Morales in Los Angeles. Ritchie needed the company of his family, and wanted to hook up in New York when Ritchie was going to be presented with a gold record for "Donna."

Bob Morales:

"He needed somebody, he said, from out here. He asked for my mom, and I told him she wasn't there. He says, 'Well, I wanted her to come down with me.' I told him she wasn't going to fly. And he says, 'Well, if she doesn't want to come I already told Bob Keane and he'll work it out for you to come with me.' I asked him, 'You really want me out there with you?' And he said, 'I want you up here.'"

The curtain came down around midnight. Buddy had called Maria in New York, but didn't mention his plan to fly to the next show. He began to assemble his sidemen for the flight to Fargo, but his travel plans started to change when the other performers got wind of his plan.

Even Ritchie, who didn't like to fly, was avid to get out of another night on the tour bus in the frozen farmland.

Tommy Allsup:

"Ritchie, all night long, would come around and say, 'Let me fly.' And I said, 'Get away from me, quit it, don't bug me.' [After the show] Buddy said 'Go back in and check and make sure we got all our stuff,' 'cause our drummer had left his hangup bag a few nights before in a dressing room. Back then we didn't have roadies, you know, we'd load our own amplifiers. So I went back in to check, and Ritchie was standing there signing autographs by a little dressing room right off the bandstand. For some reason he said, 'You going to let me fly?' And I just flipped a fifty-cent piece and said, 'Call it.' He called heads. And so I went back to the station wagon and I told Buddy, 'I'm not going to be flying. Will you get my shirts laundered?' I told him we had flipped and Ritchie had called heads."

J. P. had also heard about Buddy's charter flight and desperately wanted a seat. He was still sick with the flu. The drive to the next show in Moorhead was 430 miles, and J. P. cringed at the thought of squeezing his ailing 210-pound body into another bus seat through the night. He hoped that he could take the plane, get to Moorhead early, and see a doctor. He went to Waylon Jennings.

Waylon Jennings:

"Buddy chartered it for us, you know, because we were all tired. He was doing it as a favor to us. We could get in and get a little rest and get cleaning done. The Big Bopper then came to me. He had the flu real bad, and he asked me, 'Would you let me have your place on the plane?' I said, 'Well, if it's all right with Buddy, it's OK with me.' And Buddy said OK, you know."

When Buddy learned that J. P. was taking Waylon's seat on the plane, a good-natured exchange ensued that would haunt the young Jennings for years to come.

Waylon Jennings:

"There was a thing that happened that night. Buddy was leaning back against the wall in this cane-bottom chair laughing at me. He says, 'You're not going on the plane tonight, huh?' I said no. He said, 'Well, I hope your bus freezes up.' And I said, 'Well, I hope your plane crashes.' I was awful young, and it took me a long time to get over that."

According to some accounts, Jerry Allison and Joe B. Mauldin had met earlier that same evening at Allison's house in Lubbock to talk about the state of the Crickets. Things weren't working out the way Norman Petty had promised. In the months since the split with Buddy, the Crickets had reconfigured with old friend Sonny Curtis on guitar and fellow Texan Earl Sinks on vocals. They had cut just one single and had yet to play a single live show.

Jerry and Joe B. called Buddy's apartment in New York to clear the air, maybe hoping that opening the lines of communication might lead to a reconciliation. It was also possible that they wanted to talk to Buddy about his legally questionable use of the Crickets name. They hadn't realized that Buddy was on tour, and they spoke with Maria instead. She gave them the number of the Surf Ballroom and the hotel where Buddy would be staying in Moorhead. After they failed to reach Buddy in Clear Lake, the original Crickets left a message at Buddy's hotel and asked him to call them when he arrived.

"BUDDY WAS LEANING BACK
AGAINST THE WALL IN THIS CANE-BOTTOM CHAIR
LAUGHING AT ME.
HE SAYS, 'YOU'RE NOT GOING ON THE PLANE TONIGHT,
HUH?' I SAID NO. HE SAID,
'WELL, I HOPE YOUR BUS FREEZES UP'. AND I SAID, 'WELL,
I HOPE YOUR PLANE CRASHES.'"

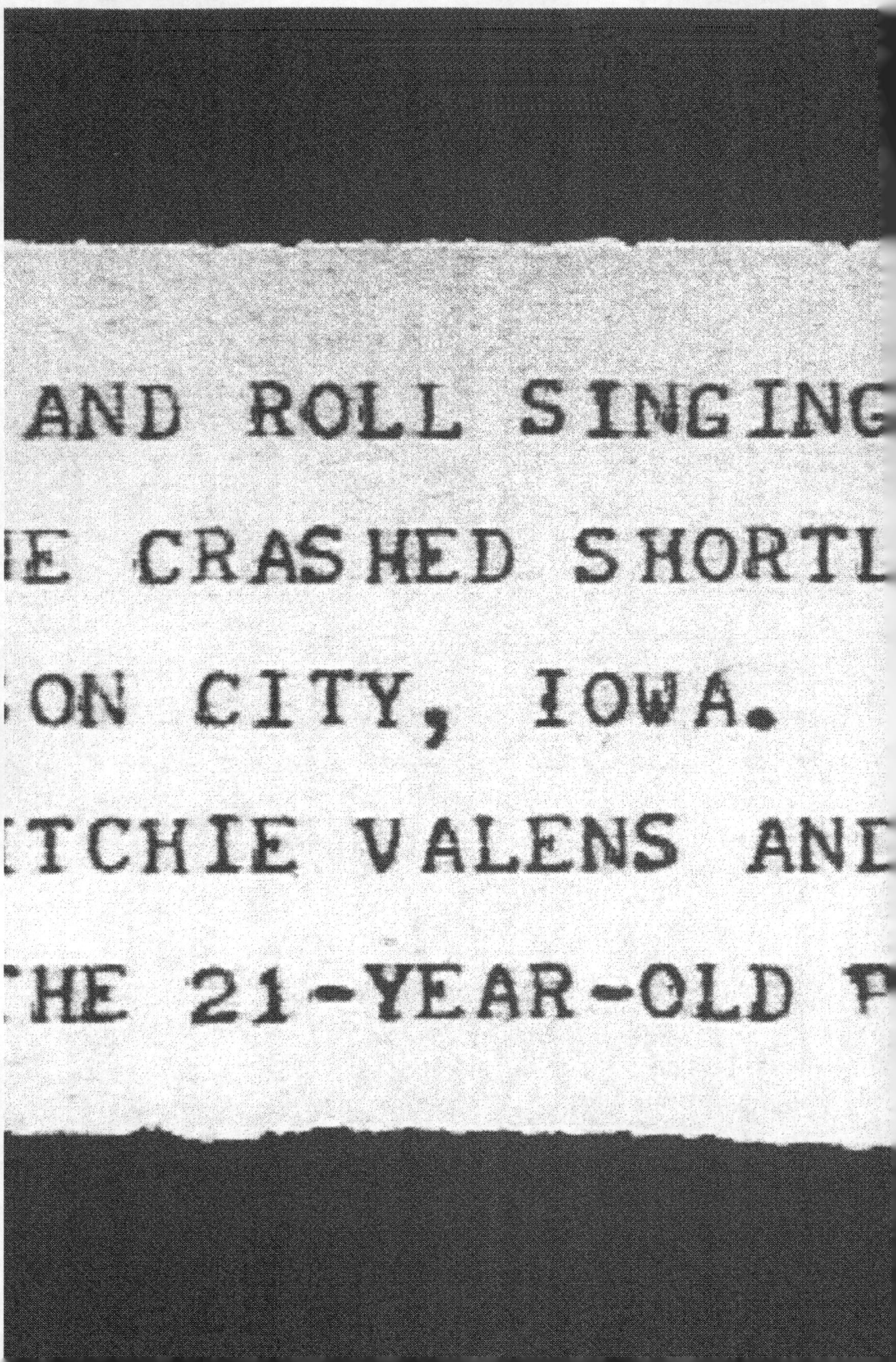

AND ROLL SINGING

E CRASHED SHORTL

ON CITY, IOWA.

TCHIE VALENS AND

HE 21-YEAR-OLD P

THE DAY THE MUSIC DIED

A *cold northeast wind was blowing in Clear Lake, and there were scattered snow flurries. Carroll Anderson, accompanied by his wife and eight-year-old son, drove Buddy, Ritchie, and J. P. to the nearby Mason City airport.*

Carroll Anderson:

"They called and said the plane would be ready, to take them right out on the runway."

Ritchie didn't like to fly, and was taking this plane only because he dreaded another night on the tour bus. Buddy definitely preferred the plane. His brother Larry was a pilot, and Buddy himself had plenty of experience flying in small craft.

Waylon Jennings:

"Buddy wanted to be a pilot. We'd flown all over West Texas when we were getting ready for this tour. We flew from Lubbock to Clovis to record. He loved flying, loved it. You'd get him talking about it and he'd drive you nuts. He would have been a good pilot, I think."

Carroll Anderson arrived with the rockers at the airport around 12:40 A.M. They were met by Dwyer Flying Service owner Jerry Dwyer and twenty-one-year-old pilot Roger Peterson. Peterson apparently had misgivings about the weather, and he had been warned by friends not to fly that night. He'd already made several trips to the airport tower for weather information and had been advised that visibility was about ten miles along the planned flight path to Fargo.

Carroll Anderson:

"I never had any concern about them flying because I've flown in weather a lot worse than that. At the airport they cleared the conditions."

Waylon Jennings:

"There was a blizzard coming. I don't know if they ever knew that. You know, that's the thing. And they flew into it. But it was very calm and everything. And relatively pleasant."

One has to wonder whether the flight was sent up in bad weather because of the determination of the stars not to end up stuck on the bus.

Waylon Jennings:

"I really can't answer that right. Now, maybe someone knows something I don't know. But I didn't see any anger or determination or anything like that. Buddy just chartered a plane. We were all tired. We were mad at the [tour] bookers, at what they were doing to us. But I don't think Buddy forced anything or pushed anything. I think he just called a plane and went. And that was it."

Buddy, Ritchie, and J. P. paid Dwyer for the flight. They said good-bye to Carroll Anderson and greeted a carload of fans who had been at the show and followed them to the airport.

Carroll Anderson:

"In the car they talked mostly about where they originated from. Ritchie Valens, it was the first time I heard him come forward, he was from Southern California. And then the Big Bopper said, 'Well, Buddy and I are from Texas and now we're going up to Fargo, North Dakota. We're getting farther away from home instead of closer.' My wife enjoyed him, and my son enjoyed him."

Then they boarded the twelve-year-old single-engine four-seat red and white Beechcraft Bonanza. Buddy sat in the front passenger seat while Ritchie and J. P. sat in the back. They were also carrying forty-two pounds of luggage, including much of the Winter Dance Party's dirty laundry, which they were going to get cleaned as a favor to their friends stuck on the bus. The load was too big to fit into the plane's luggage compartment, so some of it—including J. P.'s guitar—had to be stowed in the cockpit.

Carroll Anderson:

"We drove out to the plane and the pilot was

there and he had the engine running, and the plane was warm. The Big Bopper and Ritchie Valens crawled in the two backseats of the plane and I shook hands with each one of them as they got in. I wished them well and said have a nice trip. Buddy Holly was the last one to get in, they held the door open. I shook hands with Buddy Holly and said, 'I wish you only the best.' He said thanks. I went back to the car and sat there until they were clear of the runway."

As Peterson taxied to the dimly lit runway, he radioed again for weather information and learned that conditions had changed. Visibility had been reduced to six miles. Dwyer watched from a platform outside the airport tower as the plane took off around 12:55 A.M. Within minutes, a snowstorm hit the area.

Bob Hale:
"When they left the Surf Ballroom the stars were shining. It was a cold, crisp northern Iowa night. I was getting some records together and signing autographs, then my wife and I got in our car to drive home. We lived along the lake shore, about two miles from the Surf Ballroom. And as we're driving the snow starts to come in right across the road, right across

our lights. And I remember vividly saying to my wife, 'Look at that, the snow is incredible, it's coming straight across the road. I hope the guys got off the ground before the storm came into town.'"

Carroll Anderson was heading home with his family after a long and successful night at the ballroom he managed. But as he pointed the car homeward he saw something disturbing.

Carroll Anderson:
"It looked to me like it was a perfect takeoff. And then something happened. They got off at the far end of the runway and they were climbing. I crawled back into the car and started up, then I turned and looked in that direction and I seen the lights disappear. And I thought maybe it's the curvature of the earth or something like that, or an illusion that I had. But it wasn't. It was going down after they'd made their climb."

Once the plane had traveled approximately four miles, Jerry Dwyer also watched its tail lights descend and seemingly disappear in the distance. Like Anderson, he assumed that he was seeing an optical illusion. Dwyer was more disturbed that Peterson hadn't filed a flight

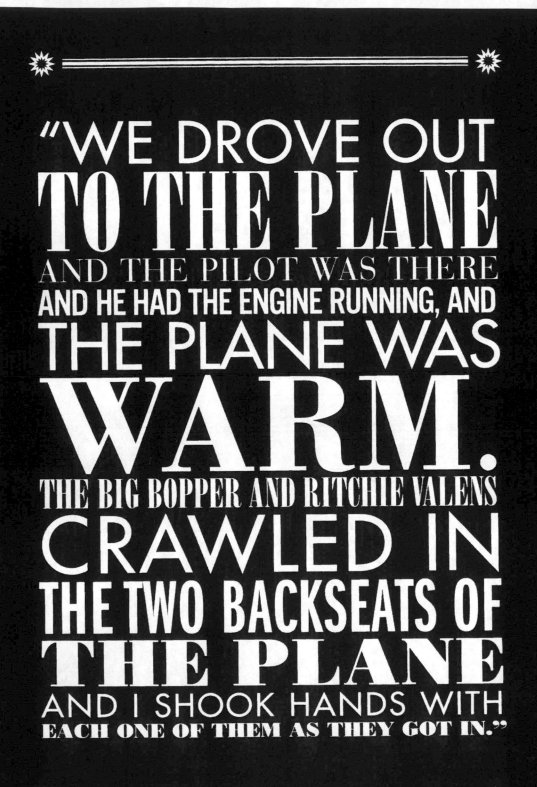

"WE DROVE OUT TO THE PLANE AND THE PILOT WAS THERE AND HE HAD THE ENGINE RUNNING, AND THE PLANE WAS WARM. THE BIG BOPPER AND RITCHIE VALENS CRAWLED IN THE TWO BACKSEATS OF THE PLANE AND I SHOOK HANDS WITH EACH ONE OF THEM AS THEY GOT IN."

plan immediately after takeoff, as he'd promised, and that the radio operator's repeated attempts to contact Peterson on the radio were meeting with no response.

Jerry Dwyer (to Civil Aeronautics Board Investigators):
"I would say it was a very normal takeoff. He broke ground about one-third the way down the runway and turned his landing lights off at approximately 150 feet of altitude. I would say the climb was quite normal and he leveled off south of the field at approximately 800 feet. This is higher than usual for a daytime pattern, but quite normal for nighttime flying. He made a 180-degree turn to the left and took up about a straight north heading."

At approximately one in the morning, Elsie Juhl heard the noise of the plane as it passed close above her and her husband Albert's farmhouse, about four miles northwest of the airport.

For the rest of the night Dwyer periodically checked in with the Mason City airport to ask if Peterson had radioed in. There was no news. At about 3:30 in the morning—half an hour past the flight's estimated arrival time—he called the Fargo airport's control tower and was told that there had been no contact made with the plane. Dwyer asked aviation authorities in Minneapolis to declare an alert for the plane. It was officially listed as missing at about 4:10 A.M.

Later that morning Dwyer went back to the Mason City airport. No word had come about the missing plane. Dwyer took off in his own craft and began to follow Peterson's flight path. At around 9:30 he spotted some barely recognizable wreckage in a snow-covered field of corn stubble on Albert Juhl's farm. Dwyer radioed the Mason City Tower with instructions to alert the police.

Waylon Jennings:
"They knocked the snow off the roof of a house about a mile back, and that plane just gradually went into the ground."

The Civil Aeronautics Board concluded that the tip of the plane's left wing had caught the ground first. It dug a six-inch-deep furrow into the frozen winter ground before being torn from the fuselage, which slammed into the ground and dislodged the passengers from their seats. The plane then struck the ground nose-first and skidded more than 550 feet across the field before hitting a wire fence. Apparently no one saw or heard the actual crash. The wreckage and its victims lay in the cold dark through the night, undisturbed save for an occasional dusting of snow.

Mason City police arrived to find the bodies of Buddy, Ritchie, and J. P. They had all been thrown clear of the wreckage. Roger Peterson had been pinned behind the controls of the crushed cabin. All had apparently been killed instantly. There was some initial confusion about identifying the bodies, since the personal effects scattered at the site included a wallet Tommy Allsup had given to Buddy so that Buddy could pick up a registered letter for him in Fargo. Carroll Anderson was woken up by the police, who asked him to come to the site to identify the bodies.

Carroll Anderson:
"We got some heavy clothing on and went out there. It was a horrible sight. I talked to the sheriff and he said, 'I don't want you to go down there because it's a pretty gruesome sight.' I said, 'It won't bother me any because I've been through some of this during my navy career.' We went back to where the first impact with the ground was made. One of the wings had hit the ground and tore out a chunk of ground about four inches deep and about three

foot long. And that was frozen solid, that ground. And from then on it was just a corkscrew. I mean they just went end over end, and it all ended up along the line fence there. All the cables were wrapped around, the tail was up in the air, and the engine was just broke away from the fuselage."

As Anderson walked the scene, his eyes found the young men who he had ridden in his car with just hours before.

Carroll Anderson:
"We seen two bodies laying twelve to fifteen feet from the airplane. One was Buddy Holly and one was Ritchie Valens. I said to the sheriff, 'Well, there was four of them in there. Where's the third one?' And across the fence about forty rows of corn in, the Big Bopper lays over there. Then we started looking for the pilot. I crawled up on top of the wreckage and

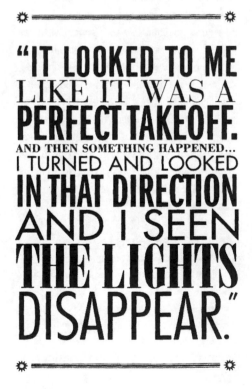

"IT LOOKED TO ME LIKE IT WAS A PERFECT TAKEOFF.
AND THEN SOMETHING HAPPENED...
I TURNED AND LOOKED IN THAT DIRECTION AND I SEEN THE LIGHTS DISAPPEAR."

there was a boot sole showing up in the mangle of the cables. So we agreed that [the pilot] was in there. We had a couple wreckers come to tear the plane apart so we could get him out of there."

Bob Hale was still unaware of the incident. He was doing his morning shift on the air at KRIB when the news came.

Bob Hale:
"The bulletin bell rang on the UPI, telling us that there was wreckage found of a light aircraft outside of the Mason City/Clear Lake airport. And I broke in with the bulletin. I didn't even think about the plane from the night before, didn't even dawn on me. I just read the bulletin and went on with music. About thirty seconds later the phone rang. It was Carroll Anderson. He said, 'Bob, I've just been out to the wreckage site of that plane you just had the bulletin on.' I said, 'Why were you there?' He said, 'To identify the bodies.' I said, 'What do you mean?' He said, 'Bob, Buddy Holly, Ritchie Valens and J. P. are dead. Their plane crashed, they're dead.'

"Back then we did not know about this thing today we call wind shear, which precedes a well-defined storm. I believe that light plane taking off was hit with wind shear and it just blew it right into the ground."

Bob Hale immediately broke into his show to identify the crash victims; then he contacted the UPI news service to do the same. He was so shaken that he had to get another announcer to finish his on-air shift.

Bob Hale:
"The phone calls started coming in from around the country from radio stations and newspapers asking for interviews. Some of the kids left school or didn't bother going to school.

"I COULDN'T BELIEVE IT. I WAS STUNNED. I WAS NUMB. LATER I DID TALK WITH J. P.'S WIFE. IT WAS DEVASTATING TO HER. HE WAS A YOUNG MAN, AND SHE WAS QUITE A BIT YOUNGER THAN HE WAS. SHE COULD SEE THE END OF THE RAINBOW WITHIN SIGHT AND IT WAS IMMEDIATELY GRABBED AWAY FROM HER."

They drove in, and college kids from Waldorf Lutheran College drove out, who had been at the show the night before. They came out to the radio station just to sit, to be somewhere to identify. And we did a lot of talking and a lot of kids crying, and a lot of parents came out to the radio station. I went over to the Surf Ballroom. It was a very emotional and very long day."

In a report filed six months after the crash, the Civil Aeronautics Board attributed the accident to pilot error, concluding that a combination of weather conditions and rural darkness forced Roger Peterson to fly blind after takeoff. He was forced to rely solely on his instruments to fly the plane. The report also found that the airport tower had failed to inform Peterson of a weather-service bulletin warning of the coming snowstorm. Dwyer told investigators that neither he nor Peterson had received information that instrument flying would be required on the flight. Peterson had

little experience flying on instruments alone. The report also noted that the plane, which was in sound mechanical and structural shape before takeoff, was equipped with an unfamiliar gyroscope that Peterson might have misread, thinking that the plane was ascending when it was actually heading toward the ground.

The CAB report didn't dispel a rash of bizarre speculation alleging that the crash was the result of foul play. A .22-caliber pistol had been found at the crash site, spawning a theory that the plane crashed after one of the passengers shot the pilot.

Tommy Allsup:
"It was Buddy's gun. I gave him the gun the summer before, when we were on tour. Because we were carrying a lot of cash. He always carried it in his little briefcase. Back then, you know, you could get on an airplane with a brief-case. If you had a gun, nobody ever looked inside your briefcase. He carried it everywhere

he went, a lot of people out West do that. He didn't have it because it made him feel tougher. That summer he was carrying a lot of cash around in the car, and I guess that was a good excuse to have one."

The handgun actually didn't turn up until the spring thaw, when Albert Juhl chanced upon it while plowing his fields. One of the gun's five chambers was empty—which fed the rumors of on-board gunplay. Albert Juhl, however, eventually revealed that he had fired the shot, curious whether or not the gun was in working order.

Another equally implausible hypothesis was that Buddy, a small-aircraft enthusiast, had tried to take the controls from Peterson.

Waylon Jennings:
"I've often wondered about that, and that's just [me being] silly. But some of the times when we'd get up in the air in West Texas, we're flying around there, and he'd say 'Let me have the wheel as soon as I can.' So there is a chance, but I don't know. But if you're twenty-one years old, and your eyes are big because you've got three stars on the plane, and the

biggest star of all asked you to let him fly, and he tells you he's got so many hours and everything—what are you gonna do, you know? What would you do? But I'm probably wrong. I don't think that's what . . . I think no matter who was at the wheel of the plane, the plane would have crashed. Because nobody was checked out on instruments."

It's very hard to imagine the ultra-sensible Buddy taking the controls of the plane in pitch darkness and in a snowstorm. Jennings's skepticism is probably well placed, although one mystery surrounding the crash was never solved: the whereabouts of a cloth bag Buddy was carrying. It contained the receipts from the Clear Lake show, at least a thousand dollars in cash.

Word of the crash was picked up by the media before the victims had been identified by local authorities, which meant that the tragedy reached the rockers' loved ones via radio and neighborhood gossip rather than through official channels.

In New York, Maria Elena Holly was in bed with morning sickness when she got a call from

MARIA ELENA HOLLY WAS IN BED WITH MORNING SICKNESS WHEN SHE GOT A CALL FROM BUDDY'S FRIEND.

Connie Lemos

Buddy's friend Lou Giordano—who told her that he was on his way over, and not to turn on the television until he arrived. But she did, and she learned about the crash from the news media. Two weeks later she miscarried her and Buddy's baby.

Peggy Sue Gerron:

"They announced it here on the radio before they even notified the family. When I first heard it I thought that somebody had made a mistake. That they had the wrong people or whatever. Jerry was devastated, just paralyzed."

Back in Lubbock, Buddy's family and friends learned about their loss in similar secondhand ways. Travis Holley wasn't even aware that his younger brother was on tour.

Travis Holley:

"I didn't know he had gone on that Winter Dance Party. The first I knew of it was I had gone home from work for lunch one time, and my wife told me, 'You better get out of your work clothes and put on some clean clothes and go over to your mother's house.' I said, 'Why?' She wouldn't tell me for a little while, and then she said, 'Well, we heard over the radio that Buddy was in a plane crash.' And I said, 'Is he alive?' I think she said that everyone was dead. And that's the first I heard of it. So I drove over to my mother's house and she met me at the door crying. She had evidently heard it too, and she asked me if it was true. And I said, 'I guess it is.' And that's the way we got the news. It was on the air before we were ever notified."

Larry Holley was out working a tiling job; he left during lunch hour to go to the site where Travis was working, only to find it deserted. After driving home and not finding his wife, he went to a nearby cafe. It was there that he heard about his brother's death. He went to his parents' house, which was surrounded by the cars of family and friends who'd already arrived to grieve with and comfort Ella and L. O.

For several hours that morning, the news reports were unclear and contradictory. In Lubbock the victims were reported to be Buddy and his band—which some took to mean Jerry Allison and Joe B. Mauldin. In Clovis, Norman Petty got the news from an acquaintance at an Indiana radio station. The first visitor to the studio that day was Robert Linville of the Roses. He found Norman and his wife in the apartment above the studio, sobbing uncontrollably.

Jerry Boynton had just come home from his morning airshift on KTRM in Beaumont when he heard the news. J. P.'s pregnant wife Teetsie was staying with relatives in Louisiana when she received the news. She would give birth to her and J. P.'s second child, a son named Jay Perry Richardson, eighty-four days after J. P.'s death.

Jerry Boynton:

"I couldn't believe it. I was stunned. I was numb. Later I did talk with J. P.'s wife. It was devastating to her. He was a young man, and she was quite a bit younger than he was. She could see the end of the rainbow within sight and it was immediately grabbed away from her."

In Los Angeles, Ritchie's mother Connie Valenzuela was washing clothes on her back porch when she heard the news on the radio. She sat down in the living room and reeled from shock. A stream of relatives and neighbors began to arrive.

Connie Lemos:

"We had a schoolmate come and say, 'Aren't you Ritchie Valens's sister? Well, he's dead?' And I looked at him and I said, 'No way, my brother is not dead, you're just jealous.' And they go, 'Well, we heard it on the news.' And all day long it was like, you keep hearing this little voice and it was like, 'No way, no way. They would have come and got me, they would have told us.' And when I got home,

Mama was sitting in a chair surrounded by people. And I knew it was true."

Donna Ludwig:

"Everybody [at school] was quiet. Everybody in the campus was very, very quiet. And my girlfriend came up to me, she was crying, and then I saw some other girls crying, and I thought something was wrong with her. And I took her hands and I sat her down and I said, 'Diane, what's the matter?' And she blurted out, 'Ritchie's dead, Donna.' At first I thought it was a joke, but it wasn't a joke. It was like somebody slapped me in the face, or hit me in the stomach. I walked right up to the public phone, called Connie's house. Ernestine answered the phone, and she was crying. And I said, 'Oh, no.' She said, 'We don't know yet, Donna, there's no positive I.D.' I tried to get out of school, but they wouldn't let me out. So as soon as I could get away from campus, I got in my car and drove over to the house. And when I drove up, there were all the camera crews, and the media, and hundreds of people all over the lawn and down the street. I snuck in the side door, and Connie was sitting on Ritchie's bed just in shock. They had her on sedatives, and the little kids were wandering around, they didn't know what was going on. It was devastating. I had nightmares for months."

Bob Keane had spoken to Ritchie the night before. He assumed that Ritchie was leaving the tour and returning home.

Bob Keane:

"I had KWFB on, and just as I passed the Palladium, I'll never forget it, the disc jockey said 'And now, the late, great Ritchie Valens.' And it was like somebody had hit me in the stomach with a baseball bat. It took me, like two minutes to get to the office, and there were all photographers there, newspaper people and everything."

Ritchie's family was shocked and devastated. His mother had a nervous breakdown, and the younger children were sent away to live with friends.

Connie Lemos:
"I kind of made myself believe that Ritchie just had amnesia, he had gotten up, he had walked away. Some farmer had found him and he was going to come home sometime. For years I couldn't listen to his music or even keep a picture of him in my house. Because it reminded me that he wasn't there."

Bob Morales:
"I was working on my car. And our neighbor came over and says, 'I just heard on the radio that Ritchie Valens and Buddy Holly and the Big Bopper had got killed.' I just started thinking that I'd better go see my mom. And I jumped in my car and went for about a block and a half. And it died on me. So I just left the car parked where it was and I ran the rest of the way over to the house. And when I got there, there was two of Ritchie's friends on each side of my mom. And my mom looks at me and says, 'We lost your brother.' Even after a couple of years, we didn't talk about Ritchie and the accident."

Later that morning the remaining players on the Winter Dance Party were met with a grim reception when they arrived at their hotel in Moorhead. They had been out of communication during their long icy trek on the bus from Clear Lake.

Tommy Allsup:
"We go to Fargo the next morning, and the road manager and I walked into the hotel. I said, 'Put me in a room next to Buddy Holly.' And there was a TV in the lobby, and there was a picture of the Big Bopper on TV. [The clerk] said, 'Are

Waylon Jennings

you with that show?' And I said, 'Yeah.' He said, 'Well, didn't you know those guys got killed in a plane crash?' So that's how we found out about it. We went back on the bus, and I woke up Waylon and told him about it. And it was just—bam, we knew about it. Kind of hit us in the face with it."

Waylon Jennings:
"I had been asleep most of the night. And I had gotten up and walked toward the front and sat down where Tommy was. Well, the tour manager come to the door and he said, 'Waylon come here, I need to talk to you. I need to tell you something.' And there's something in my mind that I didn't want to hear it. I said, 'No.' And I had no way of knowing, but I knew something was bad wrong, just from the way he said that. And Tommy said, 'The guys didn't make it. The plane crashed.' So I went in the hotel and I could see across the room. The newspaper, I could see the picture a little bit. You know, it was saying

that they were killed in a plane crash. But I wasn't going over there. So I walked around, I don't know for how long. Finally I had enough sense to call home. When I called, my mother and my family all thought I was in the plane."

Despite the deaths of its three main attractions, the Winter Dance Party rolled on. Tommy Allsup and Waylon Jennings initially demanded to be let off the tour, but the booking agency promised to give them a raise and fly them to Lubbock for Buddy's funeral. Neither promise came true.

Tommy Allsup:

"They conned me and Waylon into finishing that tour. Waylon and I called New York City and talked to this guy that was the head of GAC, and he said, 'Tommy, the show must go on.' He said, 'If you and Waylon leave, the tour's going to break down.' He said, 'If you go ahead and finish it, we'll send in some people to finish out the tour. And we'll pay you guys what we was paying Buddy.' So we thought, well, OK, we'll go ahead and finish the tour. After the tour we had a big meeting over at GAC in New York City and they said, 'Well, there's no money coming, we advanced Buddy money before the tour,' and blah blah blah."

Waylon Jennings:

"The people at GAC promised to give each one of us a lot more money to stay. And they would give us first-class tickets home for the funeral if we would stay and play. We finally decided to do it. But they didn't send us back for the funeral. It was a very cold thing they did."

One of the two scheduled Moorhead shows went on. Jennings reluctantly stood in for Buddy. He sang the songs of his friend, who had died less than twenty-four hours before.

Waylon Jennings:

"I just wanted to go home. I'd never faced anything like that. I'd never known anyone that close who had died."

Jennings adds that, after the show, the promoters tried to hold back on Buddy, Ritchie, and J. P.'s share of the pay—which they had promised to surrender in order to get the show on stage.

Waylon Jennings:

"I got kind of drunk that night, so I told them, well, if they want one stick of wood standing in the building, you tell them to pay us, or we'll tear this place completely apart. I don't know whether they finally just had a change of heart after that, but we got our money."

The next night, in Sioux City, Iowa, the tour was joined by new performers. The Winter Dance Party trudged on for another two weeks through the Midwest.

Larry Holley chartered a plane and flew to Clear Lake to identify his brother's remains. He was a tough former Marine, but he couldn't bring himself to view his brother's mangled body.

Larry Holley:

"After Buddy died, I didn't listen to the radio for maybe ten years. I just couldn't."

In Los Angeles, a community that had been galvanized by Ritchie's rapid success also pulled together to say good-bye to him. More than a thousand people went to Ritchie's funeral at San Fernando Mission cemetery.

Gil Rocha:

"It was one of the biggest things that ever happened in our little town. His family was all there, all his friends, other friends, people from out of state. The Silhouettes were the pallbearers. We had to wait for half an hour for all the people to get in."

In Beaumont, Texas, there was also an outpouring of public grief and affection for J. P. Richardson. He was interred in the Beaumont Cemetery on February 5.

Jerry Boynton:

"I've never seen a city come together and grieve the way that town did. He was so well-known there, and so well-loved. There was a sense of loss that was beyond what I could describe, and it lasted quite a while. There were memorials that were put up around the city for him."

Buddy's took place that Saturday in Lubbock. Maria flew in, but couldn't bring herself to attend the service or visit her husband's grave. Buddy's pallbearers were six of his closest musical friends: Jerry Allison, Joe B. Mauldin, Niki Sullivan, Bob Montgomery, Sonny Curtis, and Phil Everly. The service was performed by the same pastor who married Buddy and Maria Elena five months earlier.

Niki Sullivan:

"There were probably eighteen hundred people at the church. It seemed like the whole city turned out for the funeral. They expected twelve hundred and it was far in excess of that. Lubbock was very quiet that day, very respectful."

A sense of mourning was shared by rock 'n' roll fans across the country. The harsh reality of death had suddenly intruded on rock music, and the loss of three of the music's biggest stars caused many to assume that rock 'n' roll was on the wane.

Bill Griggs:

"Heroes aren't supposed to die. You know, you have movie heroes, and music heroes. And they're supposed to be there forever. It hit us

real hard. Very, very hard. It was the first rock 'n' roll tragedy. We've had a lot since. But that was really the first one."

Niki Sullivan:

"With the death of three people in the first wave, as we'll call it, of rock 'n' roll, to have three people lost, what happened to the music? Well I can tell you what happened. As of 1978, three-hundred and fifty artists had recorded our music. The number is double that now. That's the legacy that was left. That's the effect that the music had on the business itself. Buddy Holly's music communicated directly to people. It was simple music. Easily learned, easily memorized, but always happy, upbeat, danceable, it was everything that music was supposed to be. The adulation is wonderful, but to know that the music carried on, I wish there was a way that Buddy could find out. Maybe, maybe he knows. Who knows?"

There were songs that eulogized Buddy, Ritchie, and J. P. One of the most popular was "Three Stars." It was written by Bakersfield, California, DJ Tommy Dee, and the most famous version of the tune was performed by Eddie Cochran—who was crushed by the loss of his friends Buddy and Ritchie. Cochran himself would die in a car crash the next year at the age of twenty.

For years Waylon Jennings would be haunted by his joke with Buddy backstage at the Surf Ballroom, when he said he hoped Buddy's plane would crash.

Waylon Jennings:

"It took me a long time to get over that, and feeling guilty and afraid someone was gonna know it. I only told that three or four years ago. When Reba McIntire's band was killed in a plane, I hadn't been around Reba very much, but I called her and I said, 'Now

"IT WAS ONE OF THE BIGGEST THINGS THAT EVER HAPPENED IN OUR LITTLE TOWN. HIS FAMILY WAS ALL THERE, ALL HIS FRIENDS, OTHER FRIENDS, PEOPLE FROM OUT OF STATE. THE SILHOUETTES WERE THE PALLBEARERS. WE HAD TO WAIT FOR HALF AN HOUR FOR ALL THE PEOPLE TO GET IN."

you've got a problem that's just about as big as anything you're gonna deal with, you know. The thing is, you're gonna blame yourself and you're gonna feel guilty, 'cause they're dead and you're alive.' But there's an old guy [who] made me understand more. He said, and I said [to McIntire], 'Were you the one that caused the plane to crash? Did you wish that to happen and it happened? Are you that strong? Well, then you had nothing to do with it. Because you can't bring them back, either. It has nothing to do with you at all.' So I think maybe it helped her a little."

Dwyer's Flying Service was hit with multi-million-dollar lawsuits from the victims' families; Iowa law limited damages in such cases to $50,000 per plaintiff, however, and Jerry Dwyer's insurance company paid out $150,000 and kept his business from ruin. The plane's remains became the property of the insurance company after the settlement, but Jerry Dwyer bought back the wreckage when it was auctioned as scrap. There were rumors that Dwyer had hidden the wreckage with the intention of turning it into souvenirs, but eventually he confessed that he had the twisted wreckage taken to a remote location and buried.

Shock and disbelief settled into sadness and resignation. Buddy, Ritchie, and J. P. were gone.

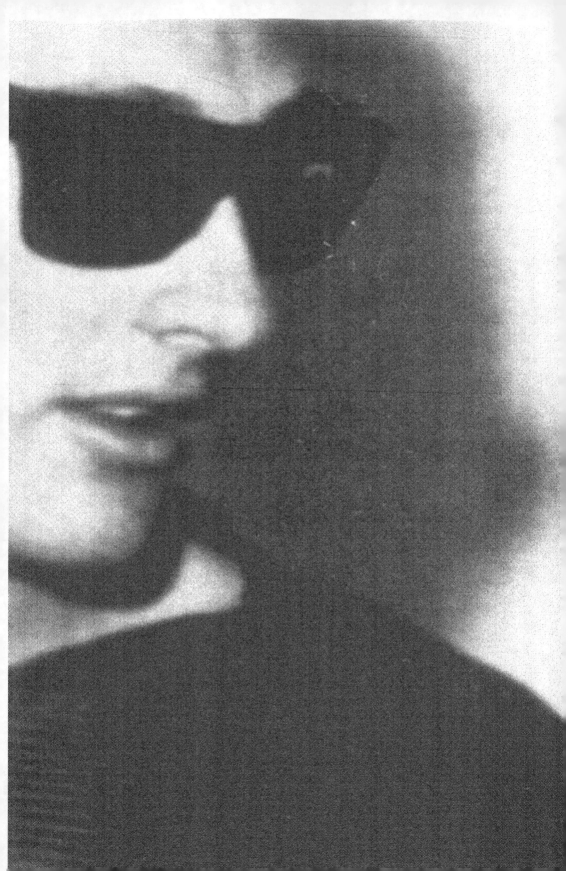

SOMEONE TO WATCH OVER YOU

✷

Four *decades after the crash, the loss of these three rock 'n' rollers still resonates. It's an image of three young heroes cut down in the prime of their lives. It was a cultural loss, and a metaphor of lost innocence and possibilities never realized.*

Bill Griggs:

"A lot of things happened between '58 and '60. Chuck Berry went to jail. Eddie Cochran was killed. I can go on and on. Jerry Lee Lewis went to England with his thirteen-year-old bride. A lot of things happened to end the rock 'n' roll era. The plane crash had a lot to do with that, but it wasn't the only part."

One of the first by-products of the crash was the record companies' realization that untimely death had marketing value. The months and years that followed saw the release of more music by Buddy, Ritchie, and J. P. than had ever been issued while they were alive.

Ritchie's eponymous first album was released two months after the crash. Another album, then a live album and greatest hits collections, followed later. Mercury Records released three more Big Bopper singles, including "Someone Watching Over You," a country-pop ballad with lyrics that seemed particularly poignant in light of J. P.'s death.

Jerry Boynton:

"'Someone Watching Over You' was released and if you listen to the words, you can construe that maybe he had a sense that something was

going to happen prematurely. But I don't think that was the case."

Jay P. Richardson:

"[My favorite] has to be 'Someone Watching Over You.' His other songs, most of them were the Big Bopper, they were zany, crazy, you know. Off-the-wall kind of stuff. But this was a heartfelt ballad, you know, it was something that came from Dad."

Two of J. P.'s compositions became big hits for other artists. George Jones scored his first number one country single with J. P.'s sly moonshine homage "White Lightning." J. P.'s Texas pal Johnny Preston also reached number one in 1960 with the novelty tune "Running Bear."

Buddy's records flooded the market for more than a decade. His current single when he died—"It Doesn't Matter Anymore"—hit number thirteen in the U.S. and topped the charts in Britain. A string of singles and LP's drawn from previously unissued material followed. This resulted in some oddities, including demos treated with newly recorded backing tracks. Eventually Norman Petty was brought back into the fold, at the Holley family's request, to oversee Buddy's posthumous output.

As the years passed, Buddy, Ritchie, and J. P. were linked by the tragedy outside Clear Lake. In the hindsight of history, at times fans lost sight of the fact that they were three individuals of varying talents and goals. Their paths ended together, but those who knew them and cared about them would always speculate about what might have been.

Jerry Boynton:
"J. P. long term wanted to write music. He would have given up performing on the stage at some point. He was a gifted songwriter, I believe, and that's what he really liked to do and that's where he found most of his enjoyment. Longer term, J. P. Richardson would have liked to see his name on a lot of record labels as the 'written by' person instead of the performer."

Bill Griggs:
"Buddy Holly, I believe, would have come back to Lubbock, built that recording studio, stayed behind the scenes as a songwriter, producing new talent, and producing records. And I don't think you'd have seen Buddy in the public eye that much. Ritchie Valens, I think, had the biggest future as far as a public star. Seventeen years old. He wrote songs, he performed songs.

I believe that as far as an entertainer, he had the brightest career out in front of the public."

The Crickets continued recording and performing in a variety of configurations, with Jerry Allison and Joe B. Mauldin filling out the band with a variety of singers and guitarists. Waylon Jennings returned to KLLL in Lubbock for a while until he started his own career as a country artist in 1965. He named his first son Buddy Dean, after Buddy and James Dean. Jennings became a major country star in the '70s as one of the most successful country "outlaws," who confronted the Nashville establishment with a rock-inspired grit and rebellion.

Waylon Jennings:
"Buddy taught me so many things in such a short period of time, about never compromising our music. He taught me about getting feeling in a record."

Jennings still blames his friend's death on the businessmen's callous disregard for the performer's well-being and safety.

Waylon Jennings:
"It still bothers me. When I think about that tour, and I think about the people who were

killed. There's no cause for that. It took the best people, I'm talking about kind, good-hearted people. They were full of life and loved life, and had great plans for the future. I've never understood that. And to this day, when I think about it, it makes me a little bit mad."

Tommy Allsup returned for a while to Odessa, Texas, before moving to Nashville to work as an A&R man and staff producer for Liberty Records; with the label he produced Willie Nelson's first solo albums. Allsup worked extensively as a session player in Nashville and Los Angeles, and in the '70s opened the Heads Up Saloon, named in honor of the coin toss that saved his life.

The Clear Lake plane crash diminished the vitality and energy of rock 'n' roll. All of the leading lights of the music were on the downside of their career, outside of the business, or dead. The edgy side of rock 'n' roll would go into hiding for the next few years, and clean-cut nonthreatening teen idols would take over popular music. Rock 'n' roll wouldn't recover until a few years later, with the rise of the Beatles and the British Invasion. The music would change, and the initial innocence and potential of the first wave of American rock 'n' roll would never be completely fulfilled.

Today Buddy Holly's stamp is every-where. He influenced the Beatles, who influenced everyone else. His horn-rimmed look has been passed down to Marshall Crenshaw and Elvis Costello. Most importantly, his formula of a winning song combined with passionate performance and crisp, innovative production and recording set a standard to which any student of the music will always aspire. Buddy had the whole package: song-writing, singing, guitar playing, and image, and he insisted on controlling the show. Many of rock's greatest performers and writers,

from Bob Dylan to Bruce Springsteen, could be described in similar terms. Buddy got there first.

Ritchie Valens left a legacy of an energized and stripped-down style. Jimmy Page has acknowledged Ritchie as his first guitar hero; Led Zeppelin were so fond of Ritchie that they rewrote his song "Ooh! My Head" as "Boogie with Stu" (though it's also fair to note that Ritchie's song owed a debt to Little Richard's "Ooh! My Soul"). "La Bamba" has proven to be one of the most durable pop songs ever, covered by countless artists in myriad styles. It would be recorded by unknown English teens Mick Jagger and Keith Richards in a 1961 living-room jam session; the tape would be auctioned off twenty-some-odd years later for $81,000.

Ritchie's music was raw and immediate. The emotions were pure: love, the excitement of youth. The songs were recorded fast and cheap, and put out on the streets as quickly as Ritchie could write them. Who knows what Ritchie might have accomplished, given the time. But there's no doubt that, in eight short months, he achieved an unrefined greatness that garage and punk bands that have come since would have to admire.

Lester Bangs
(rock critic, in *The Rolling Stone Illustrated History of Rock 'n' Roll*):
"Just consider Valens's three-chord mariachi square-up in the light of 'Louie, Louie' by the Kingsmen, then 'You Really Got Me' by the Kinks, and then 'No Fun' by the Stooges, then 'Blitzkrieg Bop' by the Ramones, and finally note that 'Blitzkrieg Bop' by the Ramones sounds a lot like 'La Bamba.' There: twenty years of rock 'n' roll history in three chords played more primatively each time they are recycled."

There is also little doubt that Ritchie forged a trail for Latino artists in the United

...BUDDY HOLLY'S STAMP IS EVERYWHERE. HE INFLUENCED THE BEATLES, WHO INFLUENCED EVERYONE ELSE. HIS HORN-RIMMED LOOK HAS BEEN PASSED DOWN TO MARSHALL CRENSHAW AND ELVIS COSTELLO.

States. In particular, Los Angeles band Los Lobos carried Ritchie's torch, and their musical explorations in the '80s and '90s took a Chicano sensibility into new creative areas.

Still, by the latter half of the '60s the music of Buddy, Ritchie, and J. P. would be marginalized by the sounds of the new generation. As the Beatles and the Rolling Stones evolved from their early rock, R&B, and blues roots, and explored new sonic and cultural frontiers, much '50s rock was relegated to the oldies bin.

Public recognition of Buddy, Ritchie, and J. P. got a major boost in 1972, when Don McLean's "American Pie" was the year's number one single. It was an eight-and-a-half minute song crammed with allusions and open to all kinds of interpretation. But at its core was

a tribute to the three fallen stars and an account of the troubled decade that followed their deaths. McLean placed the Clear Lake crash as the end of his generation's innocence and the real beginning of the '60s. "American Pie" struck a resounding chord in Americans of the time, and in the process inspired a new wave of young people to check out the music made by Buddy, Ritchie, and J. P.

Bill Griggs:
"I can look at the deaths of Buddy, Ritchie, and the Bopper as a loss of innocence. It seemed to be that period of time, things changed in this country. We lost that innocence. After Kennedy's assassination, two months later, four mop heads from England calling themselves the Beatles appeared on *The Ed Sullivan Show* and

... THERE'S NO DOUBT THAT, IN EIGHT SHORT MONTHS, HE ACHIEVED AN UNREFINED GREATNESS THAT GARAGE AND PUNK BANDS THAT HAVE COME SINCE WOULD HAVE TO ADMIRE.

literally changed music forever. And rock 'n' roll sort of disappeared after that. What we know as real roots rock 'n' roll became rock music. The attitude of the nation changed forever. We went into a war. We had civil rights, bra burning and draft card burning. The drug situation got out of hand. Yeah, the innocence was just gone. I mean, it really was."

Don McLean grew up in Rochelle, New York. As a young man he was profoundly affected by the death of his idol, Buddy Holly.

Don McLean:

"I had something awaken inside of me, feelings which were very powerful and very emotional, and they centered around Buddy Holly's music. I was fascinated with his records. ... His music saved me. He transmitted to me a whole variety of feelings which saved me, they kept me sane. And then in '59 as a paperboy, I went and cut open these papers one day. And there it said Buddy Holly and the Big Bopper and Ritchie Valens had been killed in a plane crash. I remember, it was

Buddy Holly's funeral

just like somebody punched me in the face. I just couldn't believe it. The whole time I was delivering the papers I was just in a daze."

Like so many young people of the time, McLean had felt an inner awakening and a call to euphoric freedom in early rock 'n' roll. The music urged its young listeners to revel in their youth, to connect with their turbulent feelings. The Clear Lake crash seemed to change and deepen those feelings for young America, and it is no stretch to say that the 1960s began in that remote Iowa field.

Don McLean:

"I felt so close to [Buddy]. And I never resolved the feelings that I had after his plane crashed. So one day I just began to write about this. . . . And it pointed in the direction of something else and I went there and that pointed in the direction of the rest of the song. . . . They started playing 'American Pie' and then they'd play 'Peggy Sue.' They would play 'American Pie' and then they'd play 'That'll Be the Day.' And I remember hearing that on the radio, and thinking, 'Well, this is great, this

is amazing, I'm bringing Buddy back to everybody.' ['American Pie'] saved my life, it saved my career. So, you know, I owe Buddy a lot."

Buddy, Ritchie, and J. P.'s impact on American culture was reborn in the '70s and refused to fade. A whole new generation that hadn't even been born when the three men died learned of their rock 'n' roll legacy through a pair of major hit films: 1978's *The Buddy Holly Story*, and 1987's *La Bamba*.

The Buddy Holly Story was loaded with factual inaccuracies. Jerry Allison, Joe B. Mauldin, and Buddy's other sidemen were written out in favor of two fictional bandmates, and the movie completely omitted Norman Petty. The film portrayed Buddy recording his hits in New York rather than New Mexico, showed him punching out a Decca engineer during his Nashville sessions, and showed Buddy—who couldn't read music—writing charts for strings on a recording session.

The movie showed the pastor of Buddy's family church condemning rock 'n' roll, when in fact Buddy was a member of Tabernacle Baptist Church and donated 10 percent of his earnings to the church until his death and was friendly with the church's pastor. Perhaps most hurtful, *The Buddy Holly Story* portrayed Buddy's parents as opposing his musical career. In fact, Ella and L. O. were their son's greatest supporters, and Ella is even credited as cowriter of "Maybe Baby" and "Holly Hop."

Travis Holley:
"My father especially, he dearly loved music of any kind. He couldn't play an instrument himself and couldn't carry a tune, but he loved to listen to it. And when Buddy first began, my father was behind him all the way and my mother was, too. There wasn't a doubt in their mind of what he could be, a success in it, and they pushed him, actually. Not that he needed

much pushing. They knew he was just so much, had so much enthusiasm about it, and they just got behind him and let him go and encouraged him, you might say."

Despite its flaws, Buddy's family and friends seemed to admire the film's energy—and appreciate Gary Busey's compelling portrayal of Buddy. Although some felt the movie neglected Buddy's warm and self-deprecating side, the role earned an Academy Award nomination for Busey—who sang Buddy's hits in the movie.

The Buddy Holly Story served to make Buddy an even greater legend than before. *La Bamba* did the same for Ritchie. It was a hit in theaters, and "La Bamba" became a hit again as performed by Los Lobos. The L.A. Chicano band covered Ritchie's songs on the film soundtrack; singer David Hidalgo's voice was slightly speeded up on the tapes to replicate Ritchie's timbre.

Ritchie's family had been trying to get his story onscreen for years before *La Bamba* was actually produced. Many of Ritchie's relatives appeared in the film, and they bonded on the set with actor Lou Diamond Phillips, who played Ritchie.

Lou Diamond Phillips:
"I felt this huge responsibility to get it right, to make the family feel proud that they were doing this. They had trepidations to begin with, because we were opening a whole new can of worms for them emotionally. It had taken them thirty years to get over the loss of this golden child, and here they were revisiting the places that they had lived, and seeing their lives re-created in front of them. It was very, very painful."

For Phillips, the role represented a chance to give a nuanced portrayal of a little-understood figure from rock 'n' roll's early days. He also came away with a new under-

Jay P. Richardson

standing of Ritchie's place in the history of the music.

Lou Diamond Phillips:

"It would have been highly interesting to me, you know, if he would have lived just a little bit longer, to see how he would have influenced Latino rock. I mean, today you've got Los Lobos, and Carlos Santana, and the Gipsy Kings bringing a real sort of cultural flavor to it. And everybody goes, 'Oh, yes, this is the multicultural '90s. This is the global '90s.'

Well, Ritchie Valens was well on his way to doing that in the '50s, you know? And I think that impressed me more than anything else."

La Bamba was heavily romanticized and less than completely accurate, but the movie enabled Ritchie's family to find a sense of closure.

Connie Lemos:

"With *La Bamba*, Bob and Irma and all of us were able to just finally accept, let go, just to finally be healed of all the pain and hurt and

"I WASN'T RAISED KNOWING THAT MY FATHER WAS SOMEBODY SPECIAL. MY MOTHER REMARRIED WHEN I WAS VERY YOUNG. I WAS RAISED BY A STEPFATHER WHO I ALWAYS CALLED DAD, ONLY DAD I EVER KNEW."

emptiness. I know I put Lou through some stuff. I mean, he did become Ritchie to me for those three months."

Painful emotions ran high during the filming of *La Bamba*. Things became most intense when the filmmakers shot the scene in which Ritchie boarded the flight in Clear Lake along with Buddy and J. P. Connie Lemos was on the set, and the sight was overwhelming for her.

Lou Diamond Phillips:
"She just starts trembling and says to me, 'Why did you have to go, Ritchie, why did you have to go?' And she throws herself on to me just sobbing over and over, 'Why did you have to go? Why did you have to go?' "

The period surrounding the release of *La Bamba* was difficult for Ritchie's family. His mother, Connie, was ailing. She would later pass away, but she was able to view the movie. It was the culmination of a painful period that began in '85 when the family was approached about the possibility of making a movie of Ritchie's life. Ritchie's family wanted the world to know about their lost loved one, but they were also concerned that this movie about all their lives would be accurate and tell Ritchie's story with truth and affection.

Connie Lemos:
"We had been approached before, but my mom always said, 'When it's right, it'll happen.' And when we found out that they wanted to do it, it was just chaos in our family. Everyone was running in different directions with their pain. It was really a difficult time. And I just said, 'Ritchie, I don't know what to do. Please show us what we need to do with this.' And all of a sudden it was like he said, 'You do whatever Mama wants.' I could hear it. 'You do whatever Mama wants.' So the next day I

called. Bob [Morales] answered, and he never answers the phone. I go, 'You know what? I'm fine. You know what I want to do, Bob? I want to do whatever Mama wants to do.' And he just was real quiet, and I go, 'Are you OK?' And his voice was kind of choked up. And I go, 'What's wrong?' And he goes, 'That's what Ritchie always used to say.' And I didn't know that. And then he said to me, 'It's going to be all right.' And I said, 'I know.' And from that moment on, nothing could have pulled us apart. It was like Ritchie was the glue once again that cemented it all together."

Bob Morales:
"People wanted to know Ritchie. After the movie was made, they used to come up to me and say, 'What took you so long?' My problem was, I wanted my mom to be satisfied with it. She was satisfied with it, and that was good enough for me. After the movie was over and the lights came on, my mom turned around and she looked at me. She came and gave me a hug. And she said, 'Thank you, son.'"

In recent years, Buddy's legacy has been championed by lifelong fan Paul McCartney, whose company MPL bought the rights to Buddy's song catalogue in 1982. McCartney is one of the main instigators behind the annual Buddy Holly Week celebration in England, and was the motivating force behind, and narrator of, *The Real Buddy Holly Story*, a film documentary that set out to correct some of the inaccuracies contained in *The Buddy Holly Story*.

In 1989, audiences in England were treated to the debut of *Buddy . . . The Buddy Holly Story*, a lavish stage production that re-created one of Buddy's vintage performances. The show was a surprise smash, and after a lengthy run on Broadway, was successfully staged in Canada, Germany,

Australia, Sweden, and South Africa. As of January 2000, the show was still running in London.

Ritchie remains a hero in his old Pacoima neighborhood, which includes a Ritchie Valens park and the Ritchie Valens Recreation Center—which hosts an annual music festival in his honor. The elementary school in Pacoima has a mural of Ritchie on its gymnasium wall. Meanwhile, back in Beaumont, the city is now home to the J. P. Richardson Youth Center.

In the '70s, the city fathers of Lubbock erected a bronze statue of Buddy at the Lubbock City Center. More recently, the city set up a permanent exhibition of Buddy memorabilia, and a Walk of Fame honoring Buddy and fellow West Texas rockers Jerry Allison, Joe B. Mauldin, Niki Sullivan, Waylon Jennings, and Roy Orbison.

The Surf Ballroom is still standing in Clear Lake, Iowa. It looks pretty much the way it did in 1959. Starting in 1979, the Ballroom began booking annual tribute concerts on the anniversary of the Winter Dance Party show. Vintage rock 'n' roll acts have played there, including various Crickets and the Big Bopper's lookalike son Jay Perry Richardson—who performs the songs of the father he never knew—as the Big Bopper Jr. These shows have attracted fans from all around the U.S. and the far corners of the world.

Tommy Allsup:

"It was like time had stood still. It was exactly the way I remembered it. Over on one side they made a little wing where they put some pictures and things, but it's pretty much the same as it was that night. The parking lot was still gravel, outside the back door, it was just like that night. It was kind of eerie. I met all these people that were there thirty-five years ago. This woman came up and asked me to autograph this picture that she had taken of me onstage that night."

The Surf Ballroom shows have been a personal catharsis for Jay P. Richardson. He spent much of his adult life piecing together the facts of his father's life.

Jay P. Richardson:
"I wasn't raised knowing that my father was somebody special. My mother remarried when I was very young. I was raised by a

stepfather who I always called Dad, only dad I ever knew. We didn't have records on the wall and pictures and that kind of thing."

Jay P. had to piece together his father's legacy from pieces of history and from those who knew him. It's been a long road.

Waylon Jennings:

"I'll tell you, one time I was in Houston, I was sitting on the bus. And this guy, he was about twelve years old, bounced on the bus and plopped down beside me. And he said, 'My name is Big Bopper Jr. and I want you to tell me about my daddy.' And I looked at him, you know, really shocked. Because I'd never seen him. You know, I think she was pregnant with him when the crash happened. So I said, 'Your daddy was a good old boy and a hell of a crap shooter, and how in the hell did you get on this bus?' And that was, well, we got to be friends after that."

Bill Griggs:

"The very first time I met Jay Jr., J. P. Jr., the Bopper's son, was in Beaumont. They were erecting a statue of his dad. When I walked into the room, he was in a corner talking to somebody else. He's sort of in a shadow. This man looks so much like his father, I just had to stand there for a minute, thinking, 'Wait a minute. This is the 1980s, this is not 1958.' He looks like his dad, he chuckles like his dad, he even sings like his father. I've heard him sing. And I was just amazed. And we've become good friends."

Jay P. Richardson:

"Being raised in Beaumont, these people all treated me as J. P.'s son. And when I went to the Surf Ballroom, I was the Big Bopper's son, which was a whole different thing. I never realized how he had touched people's lives as the Big Bopper. It was a very emotional weekend, to meet all those people. Until I was twenty-eight years old, I didn't know how he

actually had touched so many people."

Jay P. views performing his father's songs as a way of honoring the Big Bopper's memory, and as a family legacy.

Jay P. Richardson:

"[These were] just pretty big shoes to fill as far as I was concerned. And we talked about it and this opportunity came about a couple of years ago for me to do a show. And we got to thinking, you know, some kids, their mother or father pass on, leave them a hardware store, you know, real estate, a big fat chunk of change. My dad left me his name. And maybe a little bit of his voice. And people seem to enjoy it, so why shouldn't I be out there doing it? It seems to bring a lot of happiness to a lot of people, and it's a fun thing to do."

There have been many visitors to the Clear

Lake anniversary shows who were close to Buddy, Ritchie, and J. P. Maria Elena Holly has been there, and so have Connie Lemos, Bob Morales, and Art and Pearl Peterson, the parents of pilot Roger Peterson. In 1994, the thirty-fifth anniversary of the Day the Music Died, Don McLean performed "American Pie" on the same stage where the artists who inspired his song played their final show. Afterward McLean went back to the dressing room and wrote the words to the first verse of "American Pie" on the wall.

In 1986, Buddy was one of the first inductees into the Rock and Roll Hall of Fame. Ritchie has been nominated but not yet inducted, but in 1990 he was awarded a star on the Hollywood Walk of Fame. In 1993, the U.S. Post Office issued postage stamps honoring Buddy and Ritchie. The three young men who died in the Clear Lake crash have been bound together by the tragedy of that night. Each finds himself in good company.

In the cornfield where the plane went down, a small plaque marks the spot where Buddy, Ritchie, and J. P. lost their lives along with Roger Peterson. Fans still gather there to pay their respects every February 3.

Waylon Jennings:
"Never a week goes by that I don't think about it. I wonder what they would have been doing now."

Connie Lemos:
"You know, Ritchie is alive and well in my heart, and in the hearts of my family, and of his fans. You go to Iowa, and they don't think about the Day the Music Died. They think about how wonderful that show was."

Jerry Boynton:
"The song lives on, that's exactly right. When we go back and listen to those things, it causes us to tap our foot and really think about the simplicity of the '50s and how the '50s was a period of time that those of us who were fortunate enough to have lived through it really experienced as sort of our ground zero in our lives. A period of time that was fun and peaceful and entertaining, and J. P. brought all that to us."

Travis Holley:
"'The Day the Music Died,' they say, but the music didn't die. Buddy's not here with us anymore, but the music's still here."

Acknowledgments

Thanks to Paul Gallagher for putting in the time and pulling this together.

Special thanks to the following: Jeff Gaspin, Monica Halpert, Jacob Hoye, Dean Lubensky, Lisa Masuda, Jill Modabber, JoAnna Myers, George Moll, Mark Rothbaum, Gay Rosenthal, Ann Sarnoff, Lisa Silfen, Robin Silverman, Donald Silvey, Liate Stehlik, John Sykes, Wendy Walker, and Kara Welsh.

Presenting the companion books to one of television's most popular series!

September
VH-1 BEHIND THE MUSIC: WILLIE NELSON
Clint Richmond

The complete biography of the country music icon—from his early beginnings in Abott, Texas, to his breakthrough hits and successful songwriting career, to his involvement with Farm Aid and public troubles with the IRS, and much more!

November
VH-1 BEHIND THE MUSIC: 1968
Wayne Robins

It was a shattering year in U.S. history, filled with tragedy, unrest, and utter desperation—and along with it, artists such as Country Joe McDonald, Curtis Mayfield, Aretha Franklin, the Beatles, and Crosby, Stills, and Nash helped transform the way Americans looked at the world around them.

Available from VH-1
Pocket Books
Trade Paperbacks
www.SimonSays.com
www.vh1.com